P9-DMK-540

GRAND TETON

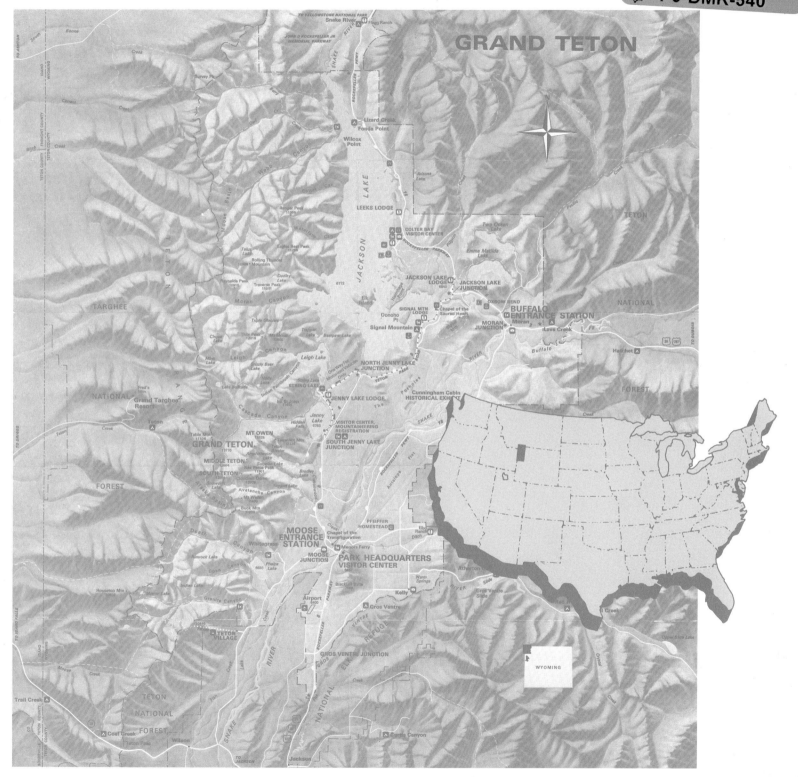

WYOMING

SEASON OF THE ELK

Published in cooperation with
the National Cowboy Hall of Fame
and Western Heritage Center,
Oklahoma City, Oklahoma
by The Lowell Press, Kansas City, Missouri

SEASON OF THE ELK

BY DEAN KRAKEL II

Library of Congress Cataloging in Publication Data

Krakel, Dean II, 1952—
Season of the Elk

Bibliography: p.
1. Elk—Wyoming—Jackson Hole.
2. Elk hunting—Wyoming—Jackson Hole.
3. Mammals—Wyoming—Jackson Hole.
4. Hunting—Wyoming—Jackson Hole
I. Title.
QL737.U55K7   75-42982
ISBN 0-913504-28-9
ISBN 0-913504-29-7 pbk.

Library of Congress Catalogue Card Number 75-42982

FIRST EDITION
Second Printing, 1977

Copyright 1976 National Cowboy Hall of Fame
and Western Heritage Center
All rights reserved. No part of the contents of this book may be
reproduced without the written permission of the publisher
Printed in the United States of America

ACKNOWLEDGMENTS

Season of the Elk would not have been possible without the interest and gracious assistance of many people. In Jackson Hole, the lives of elk and people often intertwine, and during the three-year period from inception to final product, my photography, writing and search for elk led to numerous, wonderful acquaintances and the cementing of many friendships. Because of these people, I have had many happy camps in the high country. I would like to thank each and every one personally, but until I return to the mountains printed words will have to suffice.

I was six years old when my father, Dean Krakel, Sr., first took me into his mountains—elk country. We searched for trout in his favorite streams and when I tired, he carried me on his back. Those trips first stirred within me a restless love for the wild, high country of the West. Fifteen years later, when I told him of my idea to follow the elk and to write a book, he not only encouraged me, but made it possible.

Throughout my life he has been a constant source of inspiration and help. My only regret is that we no longer have the time to walk beside the streams. My mother has always taught me that anything a person believes in strongly enough is possible. She has always been a reservoir of strength and a pillar of good judgment.

My year in Grand Teton and Yellowstone National Parks would not have been possible without the support of the National Cowboy Hall of Fame and Western Heritage Center, Oklahoma City. I am indebted to the following members of the Board of Directors: Jasper D. Ackerman, Freda Hambrick, William G. Kerr, Joel McCrea, Mrs. Nona S. Payne, J. W. Gordon, Jr., Harold Schafer, W. B. Ludwig and the late C. T. McLaughlin. They all showed special interest. The project was started during the board presidency of J. B. Saunders and concluded during the presidency of Joe H. Watt. Both gave wholehearted support. My father, managing director of the National Cowboy Hall of Fame and Western Heritage Center, outlined my requirements for the board members and kept them informed of my progress. Bryan Rayburn assisted through the Hall's accounting department.

It was my friend Mrs. Grace Werner of Casper, Wyoming, whose generous contribution to the Hall made possible my adventure among the elk. To Grace and her late husband, Herman, I owe much in so many more ways than financially.

I owe a great deal of my love for the elk to Doug and Alma Weinant of Maher, Colorado. Through Doug's wonderful stories, his careful observations of nature and his storehouse of experience and knowledge, I gained not only the basics of a mountain education when I was young, but the desire to photograph and record the beauty of the wild places and wild creatures.

While we were in Jackson, Conrad and Mary Ethel Schwiering were like second parents to my wife, Alisa, and me. Connie is a great teacher. His enthusiasm, philosophy and paintings of the Teton country were, and continue to be, a constant source of inspiration. Connie helped a great deal, not only in my field work, but in the writing and editing of the manuscript and in the selection of slides. Through his intimate knowledge of the country and people of Jackson, Connie helped me in innumerable ways. We treasure the Schwierings' friendship.

Larry and Sherry Aiuppy have been wonderful friends to us. Larry was my companion on many trips into "grizzly country." A professional mountain guide, Larry shared freely his knowledge of the Jackson Hole country, wilderness travel and survival. As a photographer, Larry was an outstanding teacher about the qualities of film and light, and a patient viewer of the 8,000 slides I eventually amassed.

We spent many pleasant evenings and had some wonderful field trips with John and Doris Clymer of Teton Village. It was John who took me for my first close-up view of bighorn sheep. I wish that all people could share the Clymers' zest for living and

their enthusiasm for wildlife and the Teton country.

Many thanks are owed the people of Jackson. Everyone I approached was helpful and gave freely of his time and knowledge. Of special consideration are Slim Lawrence, Margaret Murie, Gene Downer, Frank Calkins, Rodella Hunter, Almar Nelson, Jack and Ellen Dornan, Senator Clifford P. Hansen, Franz Caminzind, Jean Kirol, Harold, John and Donald Turner and their hunting camp employees—Lewis, Jim, Press, Tom, Ed and H. A., and the hunters who tolerated my stay in their camp—especially George Foty. Jackson outfitter and guide Larry Moore runs the sleigh concession on the National Elk Refuge and took me out on some extremely cold and blizzardy days. The driver of his second sleigh, Bob Johnson, spent many long minutes maneuvering his sleigh into position for good pictures and was always patient in waiting for me to run out of film. Jerry Hartner, as fine a camera repair technician as can be found anywhere, kept my cameras working despite the abuses to which I subjected them.

Everybody in the various governmental agencies I approached was helpful. On the National Elk Refuge I owe special thanks to Don Redfearn, refuge manager, biologist Buzz Robbins and the feed truck driver, Bob Rowley.

Members of the Wyoming Game and Fish Commission were most helpful and I owe special thanks to Pete Petra and James Yorgason. In Grand Teton National Park, this book was begun during the superintendentship of Gary Everhardt, now director of the National Park Service, and completed after Robert Kerr became superintendent of the park. I owe special

thanks to chief naturalist Chuck McCurdy and Bob Wood.

I did portions of my photography in Yellowstone National Park and am grateful for the encouragement and helpful advice of former park superintendent Jack Anderson. Glen Cole, Yellowstone biologist who for many years studied the elk in Jackson Hole, gave me helpful information as did Doug Houston. George Gruell of the United States Forest Service offered early assistance and encouragement.

This book could not have been done without the wholehearted support and encouragement of my wonderful wife, Alisa. She was, and is, my constant companion. While in Jackson, our son, Dean Wayne, was born—an added bonus.

I wish to thank Payson Lowell and the entire staff of The Lowell Press. Without Payson's enthusiasm, energy, personal touch and vision of the final product, this book would not have been possible. Doug Petty did the final editing and Dave Spaw designed the book.

Bob Scriver of Browning, Montana, read the final manuscript, offering the benefit of his many years of close observation of wildlife.

CONTENTS

1. IN THE BEGINNING

In the beginning there was ice. For millenniums the frigid climate of the northern hemisphere had been drawing moisture from the air and freezing it. Inch by inch, layer upon layer, the ice had grown until it covered the arctic in great mountainous sheets, in places two miles thick.

Two million years ago the ice began to move. Four times during the ensuing thousands of years, glacial ice would grind southward across the continents in the most awesome display of force since the earth's creation. The glaciers fed ravenously upon the land, their icy teeth pulverizing and chewing to fine dirt all that stood in the way. That which it could not destroy, the ice enveloped, swallowed whole and molded to suit its unthinking will, then moved on.

In the ice's wake animal species were forced to migrate. One of these species, although it bore little resemblance to the small cat-like creature with long saber-like teeth from which it had evolved during the preceding twenty-five million years, was the animal that became known as the elk.

Pushed out of Asia, the land of their dim dark beginnings, the different varieties of elk began moving, drifting, scattering to distant corners of the globe. Some fled to present day Mongolia, Tibet, China and Europe. Others struck out toward North America.

As the ice built up, it had drawn water from the oceans, causing them to lower several hundred feet. Whole continents that had lain buried under the seas were revealed. Such a land mass existed between what is now Siberia and Alaska, linking the two continents with a land bridge. Across this bridge and down into Alaska poured hundreds of different animal species seeking refuge from the oncoming ice, among them the forerunners of today's caribou, bighorn, grizzly, bison and elk. When the ice age ended and the last of the ponderous glaciers retreated northward, their melt water flowed back into the sea and the water level rose once again, covering the land bridge for the final time. The elk were sealed off in the new world.

Eventually the elk left Alaska and moved

To stand among the steaming morning mists, to watch storm clouds billowing over the mountain ranges and feel cool, rain-scented winds rush down from the heights is to see the earth as it has been since time began. Such scenes rekindle ancient emotions within men and whisper to them of feelings long since dulled by the concrete of sidewalks and cities.

Rays of mist and sunlight stream through lodgepole pines.

Some thirty million years ago, the Tetons were thrust upward through the earth's crust, emerging as a solid block of granite to be sculpted through the ages by ice, fire and wind. The highest peak, Grand Teton, towers 13,766 feet above sea level. To the early Indians, the Tetons were known as the "Hoary-Headed Fathers," "Three Brothers" and "Tee Win-at," meaning "Three Pinnacles." Later, French Canadian trappers termed them "Trois Tetons," or "Three Breasts." Pioneers moving westward called them the "Pilot Knobs." Eventually "Tetons" came into common usage and was officially recognized.

southward, fanning out across the lower North American continent. For thirty thousand years, before the coming of the white man, elk were the most numerous and widespread of all deer species found on the North American continent. Estimates of their number range upward to ten million, although no one will ever know exactly. Six distinct elk subspecies—the Eastern (Cervus canadensis), Rocky Mountain (Cervus nelsoni), Roosevelt or Olympic (Cervus roosevelti), Tule (Cervus nannodes), Manitoba (Cervus manitobensis) and the Merriam (Cervus merriami)—thrived in great herds in the pine forests, coastlands, deserts, rain forests, mountains and plains of all but seven of our present-day states. The name was not "elk" then, but Mus-Koose, Eh-kahg-tchick-kah and Wapiti, all Indian names. Only Wapiti, a Shawnee word meaning white deer or light-colored, has survived the rigors of time to enjoy a limited popularity.

To the Indian, Wapiti was good medicine. Among the tribes he was revered; a symbol of nobility, pride and passion. He was thought to be endowed with medicinal and romantic powers. He was credited with the creation of the earth, the power of speech and the ability to summon the gods and winds for assistance. Warrior societies were named after him. He was seen in visions and men took their names from him.

Like the buffalo, Wapiti's material uses were numerous. His meat was tender and delicious. Parts of his antler, when ground, often became a potion for healing, or when placed in a medicine bundle, brought protection from enemies to its bearer. Antlers were fashioned into implements and used in headdresses. Hides were made into robes, shirts, dresses, leggings, mocassins and calendars. Little was wasted.

White men called him "elk." They, too, marveled at this majestic member of the deer family. From the time of the colonists' arrival on the eastern seaboard, and throughout the westward movement, one finds mention of the elk and reference to his beauty and great numbers in journals, diaries and legend. Here are but a few:

"They usually accompany the buffaloes, with whom they range in droves in the upper and remote parts of Carolina, where as well as in our other colonies, they are improperly called elks. The French in America call this beast the Canada Stag. In New England, it is known by the name of the 'Grey Moose' to distinguish it from the preceding beast, which they call the 'Black Moose'."—Mark Catesby, *The Natural History of Carolina*, 1754.

"Elks and deer had traversed the prairie in all directions and trodden many paths to the river. The prairie extended without interruption as far as the eye could reach; it is called Prairie a la Corne le Cerf, because the wandering Indians have gradually piled up a quantity of elks' horns till they have formed a pyramid sixteen or eighteen feet in diameter. Every Indian who passed by makes a point of contributing his part, which is not difficult because such horns are everywhere scattered about; and after the strength of the hunting party is marked with red strokes on the horns they have added to the heap, all these horns of which there are certainly a thousand piled up. The purpose of this practice is said to be a

medicine or charm by which they expect to be successful in hunting. Elk horns are everywhere scattered about, and it would be easy to make of them a second pyramid like the one already mentioned."—Maximillian, Prince of Weid, *Travels in the Interior of North America*, writing of his visit to the Great Plains in the vicinity of the Dakotas, 1832-34.

"Turning suddenly round, I saw spread out at our feet some four or five hundred feet below us, and perhaps half a mile off, a plateau on which were grazing a vast number of Wapiti. Sitting down on a convenient rock, I had a long look with my glass endeavoring to get some correct estimate of the number . . . . There were three large groups, each of about four or five hundred, and each again divided into smaller bands. They were moving slowly westward, grazing as they proceeded. It was a grand sight, especially to one who had never before witnessed the like."—Wm. A. Baillie-Grohman, *Camps in the Rockies*, writing about a hunting trip on the plains of Wyoming, 1872.

White men so revered the elk, that in their admiration of him they slaughtered him. They sold his meat to markets, made rugs of his hide, and watch fobs of his teeth, hung his antlers on their walls, turned his grass to crops, his wintering grounds to cities and his migratory trails to roads. Within the short span of three hundred years, two of the six North American varieties, the Eastern and Merriam, were extinct. A third, the Tule, existed only as a pair of elk in captivity. The millions had become thousands, these surviving only because they existed in the most rugged,

most inaccessible portions of the Rocky Mountain West. The largest remaining herds of elk were found then, even as they are today, in northwestern Wyoming's Teton and Yellowstone country.

Today, roughly 40,000 elk call the mountainous northwestern corner of Wyoming home. This large number of elk is generally divided into two groups, the Northern and Southern herds. The Northern herd is found in the central and northern portions of Yellowstone National Park and winters along the Madison, Firehole, Gallatin and Lamar Rivers. The Southern herd is found in the lower third or southern portions of Yellowstone Park, the adjacent area known as the Teton Wilderness, the whole of Grand Teton National Park, and portions of Teton, Bridger and Grand Targhee National Forests. Each herd numbers about 20,000 animals.

Every winter, driven out of their high summer mountain ranges by deep winter snows, as many as 9,000 of the Southern herd migrate, some as far as seventy miles, to the lands of the National Elk Refuge near Jackson, Wyoming. Here in the area surrounding Jackson, known as Jackson Hole, is their historic winter range. When spring comes the elk once again migrate, leaving the refuge to follow the receding snowline back into the high mountains. There they spend the summer.

These elk comprise the largest herds of elk remaining in North America. Their historic migration is the last of its kind, equaled among hoofed mammals on this continent only by the caribou. The mountains near Jackson Hole and the 23,000 acre refuge is the herd's final stronghold.

Winters are long in Teton country and growing seasons short, lasting an average of about three months. When the snow leaves at last, the meadows and forest floors burst forth in a bright array of wild flowers. One of the most beautiful is the wild flax.

The mountains surrounding Jackson Hole are also the birthplace of one of the West's mightiest rivers, the Snake. Perhaps named for the Snake Indians as much as its twisting, coiling channels and treacherous personality, the Snake is Jackson Hole's major river. From a small lake in the southern portion of Yellowstone National Park, it flows southward through Jackson Hole to eventually join the Columbia River and empty into the Pacific Ocean on the northwestern coast.

2. THE BOY AND THE BUGLE

My love for elk began as a small boy on the last evening of a pack trip into the mountains of northwestern Colorado.

It was dusk, the cold still dusk of the high mountains in late autumn. The first snow of the season had fallen that day. Traces of clouds wandered smokelike among the ridges. A steaming mist rose slowly from the valleys. For as far as the eye could see, water reflecting the last lingering rays of sunlight flashed and shimmered like tiny bright pieces of fallen sky.

The old man and I sat on a log, warming our hands over a small fire of crackling pine branches. Every few minutes I'd take the tin cup filled with hot coffee, blow on it and noisily take a sip. Sometimes the old man would poke the fire with his walking stick. But mostly we just sat, the old man and I, staring off into the distance, our breath emerging in frosty white clouds.

There weren't many places in those mountains that the old man hadn't been in his seventy years. Sometimes in the evenings after supper, as we sat on the high ridges where the old man preferred to camp, he would point out a certain rocky ledge or patch of timber and tell me a story about something that had happened to him there. But that night he was silent, with a misty, far-away look in his eyes.

There are many things I remember about that night. The pineshadows, their jagged silhouettes creeping out across the land like boney fingers, snuffing out the last traces of the day. The first evening breezes rattling among the yellowed aspen leaves and gently rippling the small lake just below us as if someone had thrown a small pebble. The croak of a raven and the tinkle of a packhorse's neck bell, friendly sounds during the day, sounding mournfully lonesome in the twilight. But most of all, I remember the eerie, quavering whistle that rose out of the darkness. The shrillest notes seemed to climb above the trees and mountains to touch the stars, while the lowest notes rumbled in the distance like thunder boiling beneath the earth's crust. In seconds the sound was gone, lost to faint imitations of itself playing against the canyon walls. When the last of the echoes

I lay among grasses that had never been cut, stood upon high places that met the sky and was humbled by great vistas.

faded to silence, the old man and I sat unmoving on the log, warming our hands over the fire. The night seemed very dark, very quiet and very cold.

The old man sat for a long time looking off into the night. Taking long draws on his cigar, he let the smoke wisp slowly upward to curl out from the brim of his hat.

"Elk," he said, not to me in particular, but just aloud to himself and to the night.

From the way he spoke, I knew the sound was important to him. I knew, too, that it was important to me. It was as if I had heard something sacred. Something that would forever belong only to the misty dusk, the autumn mountains and to the old man and me. The bugling of a bull elk, I thought, was about the most magnificent sound I had ever heard.

The old man had seen lots of elk in his time. As I sat shivering with the collar of my jacket turned up and wrapped in an old blanket, he told me stories about them. Years ago at night, when he was out looking for cattle lost in a winter storm, he had seen phantom elk. Trotting silvery white against the snow, their breath and coats steamed with cold in the moonlight.

He had watched two bulls battling in the middle of a beaver pond. They were slogging back and forth, dripping with mud, their antlers and hooves churning the water into a froth.

Once, he had found a little bull calf with its mother strangled in a barbed wire fence. He took the calf home and raised it until it was three. One fall the young bull herded up his milk cow and left for the hills. When he tracked them down, the bull wouldn't let the old man take the cow back home.

The bull charged and the old man was forced to shoot it.

He told me of counting three hundred elk in an open basin not far from where we were camped.

"But, that was twenty years ago," he said. "The elk aren't around much anymore. Maybe a few handful still live on, but not many. Not like it used to be. Maybe up in Wyoming. You want to see elk, that's the place to go. But one of these days they'll be gone too."

I didn't sleep that night. I lay in my blankets staring into the fire's embers. The bull's fluting notes and the old man's words echoed in my memory, filling me with feelings of mystery, wildness and sadness that I have never forgotten.

The old man is gone now. The elk have disappeared and the mountains we camped in have been subdivided into lots with condominiums and Swiss-styled chalets that perch precariously and obscenely on the ridges and along the streams. But, the feelings of that night and the excitement that captured the spirit of a young boy hearing his first elk bugle have remained. I still feel the strong pull of those high ridges and yellowed meadows.

Ever since hearing the old man's mention of "Wyoming," I wanted to go there and see for myself the last great elk herds and, perhaps like my old friend, count three hundred elk in an open basin. During a summer vacation from college, some seven years later, I left my home in Oklahoma City and drove to Jackson, Wyoming, in search of elk. I did not go to hunt, photograph or study. I had no purpose in mind but to see them.

At dawn, amid the ever-present mists, a solitary, grazing bull curiously lifts his head to watch us pass. Protected within the boundaries of a national park, the bull has never learned to fear man and appears undisturbed by our presence. Some say this acceptance of man by a wild animal is "unnatural." Perhaps so, but the experience is nevertheless thrilling and becomes more natural with each passing encounter.

3. ELK COUNTRY

The elk country of northwestern Wyoming is best reached by traveling westward on highway 287 from Casper. One drives for three hundred miles through the short-grass plains country. Here, the vastness is broken only by an occasional wind-sculpted butte. Tumbleweeds bounce and career across the road, driven by howling winds which roam unchecked across the immensity. The air smells of sagebrush and sun-baked dirt. Often the great hawks, and sometimes a golden eagle, pass high overhead on motionless wings, wheeling and spinning on the thermals until they become small specks silhouetted against billowing clouds and azure skies. Occasionally, antelope, white rumps flashing in the sunlight, race alongside the car only to veer off after a few moments as if tired of the game, and string out into the distance.

Gradually, the plains give way to red, rolling hills. Snow-whitened mountains shimmer like mirages on the horizon. Just out of Dubois, the highway begins to climb toward Togwotee Pass. Sage gives way to grassy meadows and stands of aspen trees.

Wild flowers and mist-shrouded meadows are among the kaleidoscope of sights to be found in elk country.

18

Predator, scavenger and singer of dawn and dusk, a coyote, resplendent in winter coat, pauses during his search for mice.

Lodgepole are the most common of the pines found in Teton country. Their trunks are slender and straight, growing to a height of 75 feet. Indians used the youngest of these trees for teepee poles, hence the name "lodgepole." Because of their height and shallow root system, these pines are extremely vulnerable to high winds. Growing naturally in dense stands, the trees are normally protected, but recent lumbering and clearing operations have exposed them to the forceful winds which can knock down hundreds of the pines at a time. During a storm in 1973, the lodgepole forest near Jenny Lake Campground was almost destroyed.

The air suddenly becomes edged with a thin, dry coldness. Streams and rivers become narrower and water does not flow lazily, but churns and gushes downward. Stands of pine crowd the twisting road. Suddenly, just past the summit of Togwotee Pass and around a corner, although more than sixty miles away, the Teton mountain range looms on the horizon. A glimmering vision of massive rock and jagged, snaggletooth ridges thrust from the earth and stretching to the sky, the result of some thirty million years of sculpture by wind, fire, ice and water. The eye moves over them, down them, finally retreating in search of a comparison, perhaps a man-made object with which to identify. There is none.

Between the eye and the mountains, an ocean of pine forest stretches to every point of the compass. Timberline ridges dip and plunge like waves, their crests the white of unmelted snow. In every direction the eye turns, the green sea continues, broken only by new horizons, new vistas, and ending, always, in new mountains.

To the north, is the snow-covered Absaroka range in the land the early Indians called Mi-tsi-a-da-zi or "Yellowstone." To them, it was an evil country, smelling of sulfur with bubbling, boiling waters that shot high into the air; a place where evil spirits lurked and the white man's hell thundered beneath the ground. To the east, are the Wind Rivers, and to the southeast, the Gros Ventre. A considerable distance to the south is the Wyoming range. And always, to the west, are the sharp, jagged Tetons, and the sage and grass-covered valley below known as Jackson Hole. Much of this area is mountain wilderness—rugged, beautiful, primeval country, accessible to man only by foot or horseback.

For untold centuries this land beneath the mountains was visited only by the wandering Indian tribes, the Shoshone, Crow, Blackfeet and Bannock, who crossed it going to hunting and trading grounds. This was common land for all. The Indians loved its beauty and held its mysteries in awe.

In time, other men came to the valley;

men of pale complexions and hairy faces searching for the riches found in beaver pelts. These were the mountain men. Men whose names and deeds are the marrow of this mountain country. Such men as John Colter who, without weapons and clothing, raced for his life against the fleetest warriors of the savage Blackfeet nation; the legendary Jim Bridger, a noted story teller, who found a "peetrified" forest, where "peetrified" birds sang "peetrified" songs; and Hugh Glass who, left for dead by his companions after being mauled by a grizzly bear, crawled a hundred miles to civilization. These were the men of the Teton country. Many of them are buried here, unknown and forgotten, victims of the savage unpredictability of this mountain country.

After the golden age of fur trading, when gentlemen's hat styles turned from the felted hide of beaver to the more procurable and cheaper manufactured cloth, many old trappers returned to Jackson Hole as guides for that which they detested most, civilization. In time, the town of Jackson was built at the southernmost portion of the fifty-mile-long, eight-mile-wide valley, where the snow did not settle in so deep.

Today, Jackson is a popular, year 'round resort town catering to the millions of people who visit Grand Teton and Yellowstone National Parks. The town boasts a population of about 5,000 residents, although the summer population is considerably greater.

Just as it is impossible to separate the Jackson Hole country from its colorful history and beauty, the country cannot be

separated from its wildlife. Found here in fast disappearing numbers and diminishing variety are bighorn sheep, moose, deer, buffalo, black and grizzly bear, a profusion of smaller animals, waterfowl and birds, including the rare trumpeter swan and bald eagle.

Here, too, is the largest concentration of elk to be found anywhere in the world. For, as Theodore Roosevelt said of Jackson and its surrounding mountains, "This is home of all homes for the elk."

The great elk herds would elude me during my first brief summer visit to Jackson Hole. But I would return in search of them many times over during the next several years. My time in Jackson, however, was always hurried, always piecemeal, with never enough time to really get to know the country and the animals. I was curious about these elk. I wanted to know where they went, the cycles of their lives, what they saw, what they ate and why they are the way they are.

The history of this beautiful country and the colorful, and often controversial, epic migration of the elk have always filled me with awe and excitement. Nothing I read could satiate this curiosity; it seemed only to whet my appetite.

Then, one bitterly cold December day, while looking out over the refuge's large number of wintering elk, I knew what I really wanted to do. I wanted to follow the elk upward to their summer ranges and back down again.

In the spring of 1974 my wife and I returned to Jackson. This time to follow the elk through the seasons of their life for an entire year.

Of the many waterfowl species found in the Tetons, two of the most elegant are the Canadian goose, above, and the trumpeter swan. Millions of trumpeter swans once abounded throughout the United States. Sought by market hunters for their feathers, only 35 of these swans existed in this country in 1931. Now protected by law, the swans number about 1500. Trumpeter swans once migrated south during the winter, but when their numbers dwindled the instinct to migrate was somehow lost. The largest of all waterfowl, their distinctive brassy voices are a sound of true wilderness.

4. THE RUT

To know the elk is to know the seasons. For it is the seasons, with the grasses and snows they bring, that govern his life. The seasons bring the herds down from the summer ranges and draw them back up again in the spring. The changing seasons determine the cycles of birth and death and so, too, the seasons determine the perpetuation of the species.

If I had but one season to know the elk I would pick fall. Before the arrival of autumn, I would journey to the highest portions of their ranges and search out the secluded timberline basins and hidden forest meadows where the elk have spent the spring and summer months. Here, the air hangs heavy with their musky scent, the grasses are bent with the still-warm impressions of their sleeping bodies, the stream banks are trampled with their half-moon tracks and the ground and fallen logs are littered with their dung. Here, during the cool early mornings and evenings, herds of cow elk and their calves melt from the timber to water and feed. The cows walk slowly with heads arched gracefully high,

flared nostrils quivering, large eyes searching and ears flicking back and forth. The calves, no longer confined to long periods of rest and hiding, cavort through the herd, jumping, bucking and chasing in wild games of tag. They stop at times to sun, feed and nibble at the grasses. During the summer, winter has been forgotten. Stomachs bulge comfortably beneath the shiny red, short-haired summer coats. At times, these feeding groups of cows and calves can be heard from great distances, filling the air with a variety of whistling, barking and squealing.

Late summer finds the majority of the bulls segregated from the cows in small bachelor groups of three to a dozen individuals. The bulls feed in the cool hours of dawn and evening and spend the remainder of the day resting in the shade. Winter-shrunken stomachs have filled out. Old wounds and hurts have healed.

Since March, when they were shed on the winter range, the bulls' antlers have grown back at the rate of up to one-half inch a day. Now fully grown, the antlers are

Every year, usually in March, bull elk shed their antlers. The hard bone of the old antlers is replaced by a pulpy tissue, rich with blood and nerves and covered with fine hair, known as velvet. While in the velvet stage, the new antlers grow rapidly and by early August growth is complete. A mature bull elk's antlers may be five feet long and weigh fifty pounds, with six points on each side. Occasionally, a bull may carry seven points. The tines of the antlers sweep upward branching off in a succession of points from the main beam. Beginning at the base of the antler, the first set of points is known as the brow; the second, bay or bez; the third, tray or trez; the fourth, royal or dagger; while the fifth and sixth sets of points are called sur-royal. Seventh points are called imperial points. Although the number of points is an indication of maturity, it does not reveal the exact age of a bull, as some people believe.

Once antler growth is complete, the velvet dries and is shed by the bulls who rub their antlers in the ground and grass and against small trees. The trees are usually stripped of most of their branches and bark.

As the rut progresses, the bulls begin to wallow in the mud. If there is not a natural wallow nearby—a small pond, marsh or spring—the bull creates one by pawing and tearing up the ground with his hooves and antlers. Once satisfied with his preparations, he rolls in the mud and grass. Because of constant activity and sexual ardor during the rut, body temperatures are high. Wallowing is a means of cooling off.

still covered with the furry nerve and blood-rich tissue aptly called velvet.

In the warm, green days of late summer a subtle change is taking place in the high country. The autumnal equinox is approaching. The earth tilts its northern axis away from the sun causing the days to grow shorter and the temperatures cooler. Summer is slipping into autumn.

The elk are stirred by the urgency of fall. The shortening daylight hours have triggered within them a biological time clock. Glands responsible for the elk's sexual characteristics are stimulated by the amount of sunlight absorbed through the eyes. As the light decreases in the fall, these glands release hormones into the elk's system. In the cows this causes the start of the oestrous cycle, while in the bulls, the testicles lower and fill with semen, the neck swells, antler growth stops and the velvet dries up. Now begins one of the most dramatic and critical periods in the elk's life cycle. In these autumn meadows the generations of elk to come are seeded and the final destiny of the species is determined as it has been for a thousand autumns past. This is the breeding season, the rut.

No one knows how many other factors are prevalent in the fall environment, besides the autumnal equinox, that affect the rut's beginning and duration. From year to year, in different locations, under different seasonal conditions, the timing varies.

As soon as it dries, the bulls begin to shed their velvet by rubbing their antlers on trees and brush. When first freed of the velvet sheath, the antlers are white. Later, as the rut progresses, the bulls continue to

rub their antlers, parrying and trading blows with any small tree that happens to be handy. As the antlers are rubbed back and forth during the season, the mixture of bark, sap, dirt, mud and blood stain the antlers to various shades of brown, even to the point of appearing black. The bulls also plow up the ground in great furrows with their antler points. For twenty minutes one afternoon, I watched a bull plunge his antlers deep into the ground, buck and twist, jerk them out and toss clumps of dirt and grass over his shoulder. It is this activity that gives the antler points their ivory color.

Once the bulls' antlers are free of the velvet, summertime companions become less sociable toward one another. Although it will be many days before they seek out the cows for breeding, the bulls approach and pass each other cautiously, their hackles bristling, legs stiffened and heads arched threateningly.

I grew up reading the glowing stories of the violent, red-eyed, antler-crashing combat of rival bull elks during the rut. Every year, written accounts and artistic impressions of these duels embellish the pages of nature magazines. After many years of accepting these fire-breathing tales as gospel, I was not prepared for my first sights of elk combat.

My notes of the experience read as follows.

"August 19, 1974: Saw two young bulls, one a three-point, the other a four, sparring this morning. (The number of points refers to the number of antler points on one side of the head. A three-pointer would actually have six points total, etc.) Their antlers had just recently shed the velvet and were very white and flecked with blood. Pieces of the velvet still clung to the points like old tattered rags. An older and larger bull, carrying six points on each side and still in the velvet, grazed calmly nearby as the two jousted. Squaring off to face each other, the bulls walked together, lowered their heads and engaged the antlers, rattling them back and forth. The sound was like snapping twigs or castanets. At times, both bulls seemed extremely serious as they grunted, locked their antlers and twisted and shoved back and forth. Many times, over the course of twenty minutes, they broke apart, grazed and then resumed. Finally one bull broke away, trotted up a hillside and disappeared into the timber.

"All of the bulls I have seen today, with the exception of the one six-pointer, have shed their velvet. There are no cows in the area."

"August 20, 1974: Watched five bulls spar this morning in a small clearing. Two bulls shoved back and forth while the others watched or grazed. The combat, if you can call it that, was very gentlemanly, almost as if governed by a certain set of rules. The bulls faced each other, lowered their muzzles and walked together until the antlers met. There was a great deal of twisting and maneuvering, but no bull seemed to want to break away and attack the other's flank or rear.

"This evening I walked upon three bulls grazing in a large meadow: a very large mature six-point bull with heavy antlers, a lesser six-point and a four-point. As the large six-point bull grazed, the four and the other six locked antlers and shoved each

28

While older bulls spar with one another, a decayed tree stump makes a less dangerous, although unyielding, opponent for a five-month-old calf anxious to prove his mettle. From birth, a young bull begins the struggle for social rank and superiority. It may be many frustrating years, however, before he is able to compete with the more mature bulls for the possession and breeding of cows.

other back and forth, filling the air with a shrill whining. After three separate engagements, the four-point left the six, walked to the large bull, lowered his head and these two then shoved back and forth. Being three times as big, the larger bull could have easily flung the young bull away, or gored him and gone about his business. Instead, the two parried back and forth for the better part of an hour.

"Just at sunset, four new bulls entered the meadow. All activity of the three stopped, and they walked to where the four had entered. All stood facing each other, necks outstretched, antlers shaking, hackles raised, and then a series of sparring matches erupted. Each of the new bulls tested the bulls already in the meadow. At one time there were three separate matches going on at the same time. The air was filled with the sound of antlers lightly hitting one another, and the whining, which sounds like a trilling bird call. There was no bugling. No cows were in sight.

"The young bull tried each of the new bulls, one after the other, each stronger and larger than himself. And then, with little show and without being chased by another bull, he left the meadow and walked into the timber. By dark the six remaining bulls were grazing peacefully in the meadow."

Disappointing? I thought so. Believing that maybe the rut hadn't really begun, I waited to see the actual "combat" so often described. During the three months that I spent in the field during the rut, from August 12th to November 12th, I photographed one hundred separate encounters between bulls that resulted only in antlers being engaged. I saw many more that I recorded only in my log. Not once during the rut did I witness the legendary bloody fights. Thinking that I had missed something that a lot of other people had seen, I began researching.

In his book, *The Elk of North America*, Olaus Murie, who studied elk in Jackson Hole for many years for the U. S. Biological Survey, summed up his many studies and observations on the subject. "Interlocked antlers have been found, and battles have been described by various observers. But during the entire time of the present investigation not a single really serious battle among the elk was observed."

Dr. Margaret Altman, who is the foremost authority on the elk's social behavior, wrote in one of her technical journals, "The seriousness and duration of the fighting is generally overrated. A considerable amount of formal sparring and intimidation display takes place. The retreat of one partner, either before the fight gets underway or after a few blows, terminates the majority of male encounters."

Carolyn Barber in the book *Animals at War* wrote, "The fighting between male rivals never purposely ends in death; there is no point in this. The rightful owner of the territory or harem of females merely wants to show the intruder off the premises and employs various threatening postures and expressions to do this. These actions are easily and quickly recognized by his opponent and if the opponent is wise he withdraws without much ado. Sometimes the dispute does erupt into a fight, but even when there is apparently violent physical contact, severe damage is rarely inflicted. Fatalities do happen from time to time, however, and this is exactly why the threat of injury remains effective even if seldom carried out."

I have talked to many biologists and people who have lived in elk country all their lives. Few have ever seen the epic fights of the bulls.

The longer I thought on this subject, the more I poured over my notes and photographs, comparing them with those made by others. It became apparent that the dominant bulls which do the breeding during the rut are not selected through violent contests, but through a system of hierarchy in which combat serves as a ritual of social rank. This hierarchy governs a bull's life from the moment of birth. Thousands of years of evolution have shaped his physical appearance, habits and social order for the sole purpose of breeding.

True competition for the cows doesn't take place in autumn combat. It begins the moment a bull calf takes his first breath of

Combat among bulls during the breeding season or rut is often overrated. Fighting generally takes place early in the fall while the bulls are still in bachelor groups and have not as yet sought out the cows, or after the rut in early winter when fatigue and lack of food make tempers short. Violent fights between bulls over a harem of cows are rare, however, and death or injury is the exception rather than the rule. Combat, when it does occur, lasts normally but a few seconds.

life and wobbles to his feet, searching instinctively for the cow's nourishing milk. Should he survive the numerous predators and the inclement weather during the first few days, he will have already emerged victorious over other less fortunate bull calves that would have some day been his rivals.

In the calf's games of tag and playful butting of heads with companions, he begins the lifelong struggle for social standing. At an early age, he must be either submissive or dominant. As calves grow older and gain in confidence and size, the play becomes less frivolous. They threaten and butt vigorously or they may stand on their hind legs and strike boxer-like with their hooves.

A young bull remains with the herd in which he was born only until his second autumn. By then he has grown his first set of antlers, two long, spindly spikes varying from a foot and a half to several inches in length. The moment an older bull takes possession of the cows in the fall, the spike, or young bull, is viciously driven from the herd. His antlers have marked him an intruder, a rival. Sometimes by himself, sometimes with others who have also been driven off, he stays in the timber out of sight. Feeding at the far ends of the meadows, he watches and follows the herd, trying at every chance to rejoin them. He is driven off again and again. Given only his instincts and the keen, well-developed senses with which he was born, he must struggle for day-to-day survival. He must gain acceptance back into the herd structure and earn his eventual role. This he can do only as a mature bull.

Elk do not fear the water and are strong swimmers. In the heat of summer they will stand in streams or lakes to cool off or escape pesky insects. Elk will seemingly go out of their way to seek out water for a quick swim and a few minutes of splashing play.

With voice roaring, neck out-stretched and vicious prods of his antlers, the harem master moves his cows to a new meadow. Because there are more bachelor bulls than harems, this bull must be constantly vigilant, lest a straying cow be stolen from him. During the rut a herd bull will patrol the perimeter of his harem and make his presence known by bugling, pawing the ground and rubbing his antlers against trees.

The frosted breath of the bull at far left is visual evidence of one of the mountains' most thrilling sounds. There is no adequate means of describing the bugling of a bull elk. It is more than a sound. It is a fleeting moment in time, a multitude of sensations that well up within the listener's chest and make the hairs on his neck bristle with excitement. The bull's bugle is a wild and beautiful song that echoes a primal intent, a struggle for supremacy and survival that is millions of years old. Once heard, it is never forgotten.

By the bull's third year he stays almost exclusively with the other bulls, summering and wintering in small bachelor groups. It is here, within these groups, that the harem masters are determined and the breeding cows won or lost. Within the hierarchy of the bull herds there is a continual fight for supremacy and social rank. The fight for possession of the cows and the right to breed them takes place not only during the rut, from September through early November, but all year long. The struggle consists not only of direct contact, but meaningful gestures, postures, attitudes and vocalizations. A young bull works his way through the hierarchy by engaging in pushing and shoving contests with companions. He learns to keep a respectful distance from those larger and stronger, while dominating those smaller.

Although a three-year-old bull is sexually mature and has the desire and ability to breed, it may be several frustrating years before he is able to do so. A young bull lacks both the size and seasoned wisdom of the larger, older bulls with whom he must compete. Only the largest, strongest and most aggressive bulls will be able to take and hold a herd of cows during the rut. Competition is nature's way of insuring that only the best bulls do the breeding. The traits that have made them successful will be passed on to future generations.

During the rut, bulls change in appearance. This change is most noticeable in the larger, older bulls. The neck and hump swell to twice normal size. The shaggy mane hairs lengthen and darken. The antler beams are polished dark brown, with points whitened by the constant rubbing of trees and grass, and appear much more massive and formidable than after first losing the velvet.

Every one of these features exaggerates the bull's already massive size. Combined with aggressive behavior such as outstretched neck, raised hackles, deep roaring bugle and threatening shakes of the antlers, these features give a large bull every impression of being a formidable and overwhelming opponent not to be trifled with.

The antlers are a key part of this impres-

34

This enraged herd master vents his anger with a screaming bugle after having his cows stolen by rival bulls. During the rut, the frontal portion of a bull's body swells to twice normal size, serving to exaggerate his appearance. The combination of swollen neck, dark dangling mane, menacing antlers and roaring bugle makes this half-ton bull an awesome sight.

sion. In the distant past, perhaps antlers were designed for combat and protection. They long ago lost that primary function. For it is the female who protects the young and she lacks these appendages. The bull takes no interest in herd life, the raising of the young nor the protection of the family unit. For most of the year, he remains aloof and separate, a complacent, cud-chewing vagabond. Even if antlers were designed for the bull's personal protection, they are uselessly encased in the tender velvet for the majority of the year. The antlers, although potentially dangerous, are rarely brought into play in serious action. Bulls and cows protect themselves by standing on their hind legs and lashing out their front hooves with lethal snake-strike quickness. The antlers are a social badge. They are part of a masquerade, a bluff designed to intimidate rival bulls.

The most important factor affecting a bull's rise through the hierarchy is time. Should a young bull survive the elements and his predators to reach the mature age of six or seven years, only then, wearing the scars of the seasons, will he be at the top of the bull's social ladder. A fully matured bull, he is able to take and keep a herd of cows and take full part in the propagation of his species. Once he has outlived his usefulness, usually when his teeth are so worn down they can no longer provide him with the energies his body needs for breeding and survival, he will be replaced by younger and stronger bulls who have come up through the ranks.

By early September the bull herds have disbanded. As these lone bulls seek out the large nursery herds of cows, the mountain air echoes with the shrill calliope-like bugling, so closely identified with the bull elk and the rut.

In Jackson Hole country, the bugling of the bull elk is as much a part of fall as the flaming yellow aspen leaves, flights of geese passing overhead and mountains freshly white with snow. For many mountain residents, it is not really fall until they hear the season's first bugle. They know it means that up in the hills the bulls are gathering their harems and it won't be long until the first snow flurries of winter arrive on the valley floor.

Bugling is most closely associated with the screaming challenge of the herd bull declaring his possessive might to all within hearing range. Yet, to me, it also brings to mind the young bull I saw in early August who stood amid the mists raising his head to mournfully howl dog-like to the heavens or the old bull laying in the snows of December dreamily bugling once and returning to sleep.

Just as bulls bugle in a variety and combination of sounds ranging from grunts, whistles, barks, screams, whines, moans and roars, they also bugle for many different reasons. Every tone, note and pitch, when combined with different stances, movements and gestures, has definite meaning to other elk. The bugling of a bull laying lazily in the shade is quite different from that of one who stands with hackles bristled and antlers shaking.

In the course of my field work, I have recorded some ninety minutes of elk bugles. I have played the tapes back to a variety of bulls, sometimes using their own voices. Often, a bull will graze while the recording plays. Then suddenly a certain tone, a certain pattern of bugling evokes instantaneous anger. Several times the reaction has been so quick that I have been barely able to gather up my equipment and scramble out of the way. The same recording will evoke different responses from different bulls. A small bull will slink away. A larger bull will bugle back.

Bugling is an expression of the bull's emotions which run the gamut from anger to exhilaration. Generally, the bugle begins

as a low, deep rumbling sound within the chest. Leaving the bull's mouth, it may sound at first like a bellowing roar. Then it will climb calliope-like, sometimes dropping back down the scale three or four octaves, and most often end abruptly amid a series of coughs and grunts. At great distances, only the last, highest pitched notes reach the human ear; hence the musical, flute-like sound often described. Up close, an elk's bugle sounds like a roaring, coughing scream. Heard at night in

A weary cow, pursued for several days since coming into heat, becomes momentarily docile as she permits the bull to nuzzle her ear. Moments after this photograph was taken, however, she bit her pursuer's neck, jumped to her feet and the chase was renewed. Breeding most usually takes place in the early mornings and evenings.

the dense brush of a willow thicket, it can be one of the most terrifying sounds on earth.

A bull's age does not determine the sound of his bugle. Even in early fall, before constant bugling makes voices hoarse, I have heard the oldest, largest bulls emit only scratchy, high-pitched squeaks, while the youngest, scrawniest juveniles sound forth in mellow, full-bodied tones that would put a concert flutist to shame. Generally, a bugle lasts an average of only six seconds.

Since hearing my first elk bugle in Colorado I have heard many, many more and always the same excitement returns. There is no finer way to end a day than to lay under a blanket of stars near the warmth of a fire, and hear faintly in the distance the bugling of several bulls ringing through the chilly, fall night. It is a timeless song of the mountain autumn.

While the cows are still in the large nursery herds, the bulls seek them out and, if they are not already claimed by a larger bull, take possession of them. Many times a younger bull has moved in with a group of cows. He is run out by the larger bull and usually accepts his fate without show of combat. Even when precious cows are at stake, a small bull is not driven to heroics in the face of a larger bull.

A bull does not round up individual cows and throw them into his herd. The herd already exists. The bull simply walks in and takes over, searching out and breeding those cows in heat. The size of a bull's harem is limited only by the number of cows a bull can accommodate and keep together. The greatest number of cows I saw in a bull's possession during the rut was thirty-six; the fewest, one.

Because rival bulls will try to steal cows from the harem master, his vigilance must be constant. Cows are kept in open meadows. Fringes of the herd are always under watch. The bull constantly trots through and around his herd, testing the air, bugling, wallowing and twisting his antlers in threatening displays. Stray cows are herded back into the clearing as the bull approaches them with neck lowered and stretched and teeth clicking. With vicious prods of his antlers, the bull moves the cows.

The oestrous cycle of the cow elk lasts a total of 21 days during the breeding season. She will come into heat for a 17 to 36-hour period and if not bred during this time will come into heat again at recurring intervals during the 21-day cycle until she is bred. Once bred, she will not be in heat again until the following fall.

When a cow is in heat the hind quarters become quite swollen and the vulva red and extended. Her stub of a tail sticks practically straight out. The body secretes fluids, the smell of which announces the cow's readiness to breed. If approached by a bull during the primary periods of heat, the cow will ignore his efforts and move off. The ensuing chase is often persistent, sometimes lasting for days, and is filled with generous kicks, prods and bites. This constant activity and lack of time for sleeping and eating is exhausting for the cow and bull. Only when the time is right does the cow become docile and submit to the bull. Copulation is short. There is no lingering romance.

Exhausted from long hours of vigilance, fighting and breeding during the rut, a weary herd master rests in the shade of a pine tree and waits for winter.

During my year of observation, the rut began with preliminary activities by the bulls on August 12th. The peak of the breeding activity occurred from the middle of September to mid-October. From that time on, it subsided until early November when the migration to the lower ranges began.

As the height of the rut passes, many of the herd bulls lose interest in the cows and wander off by themselves or gather once again in bachelor groups. Here, among the other bulls that only days earlier were rivals, they graze and rest. Many of these bulls, depleted of energy and exhausted by days of fighting, breeding, chasing and constant vigilance, have lost more than one hundred pounds. Now, they feed continuously, trying to replace the lost stores of fat that will sustain them during the long migratory trek to the lower country and the lengthy winter to come.

5. THE NIGHT THE ELK CAME DOWN

In the glare of my pickup truck's headlights the elks' eyes gleamed like hundreds of tiny bright stars. Confused by the sudden brilliance of light, a dozen elk milled about on the road. Others, their dim outlines barely visible, stood in the shadows at the road's edge. Pumping the brake pedal, I pulled off to the side, shut off the lights and motor, rolled down my window and watched.

A river of elk, their shadowy forms a confusion of antlers and bodies silhouetted against the moonlit snow, poured swiftly out of the trees and darkness to cross the road in front of me and disappear into the night. More took their place, and when those had passed, still more came. Long, winding ribbons of elk were flowing from the windblown hillsides all around me. The air was alive with their movement. Hooves clicked on the road's pavement. Snow squeaked and crunched under their weight. Tree branches slid softly against their bodies. The cold night air was filled with the barks, whistles and grunts of hundreds of migrating elk.

The night sky was clear. No snow had fallen for days. What invisible force had driven these elk down? What unheard voice had whispered to them that tonight was the time to move urgently toward the lower country before the final snows of winter came burying the high country grasses beyond reach of their pawing hooves? Spellbound, I sat shivering in the night air, alone with my thoughts and the moving elk.

I was witnessing a sight few people ever see. A spectacle of primal beauty as ancient as the elk species. On other nights such as this, some ten to thirty thousand years ago, the elk, moving as they were now ahead of the snow and cold, found an ice-free passage out of Alaska and down into the lower continent. When man was still drawing pictures on the walls of caves and chipping his spear points from flint, the movement of the Teton elk was already ancient. Civilizations rose and fell while the elk continued to move with the ebb and flow of the snow seasons, migrating between their high summer ranges and their winter ranges

In advance of violent winter storms, a river of elk, nearly a mile long, flows from the high summer ranges toward the National Elk Refuge in the valley of Jackson Hole. No where else on earth do such large numbers of elk migrate over ancient trails between summer and winter ranges.

Steadily falling snow signals the beginning of winter in the high country. For many of the elk, like this lone bull that summered in southern Yellowstone National Park, the migration to lower winter ranges in Jackson Hole covers more than seventy miles.

In the midst of a swirling ground blizzard, a group of cows moves across a windswept flat toward the protection of the foothills.

near Jackson on trails worn deep from their hooves.

The elk moving in front of me had been trickling down from the mountains in small bands for many weeks. From all points of the compass, some from over 70 miles away, they had come; from upper Berry Creek near the Wyoming-Idaho line; from southern Yellowstone Park; the Thorofare country, Big Game Ridge, Chicken Ridge, Two Ocean Plateau; from the upper Gros Ventre; from the head-waters of the Snake River, the Buffalo, and Pilgrim and Pacific Creeks. From wherever the herds came, they moved with a common goal—to reach the low country before winter. As the first snow flurries turned to storms, the trickle of elk had become a stream, and then, in the last minutes before winter, the stream had become the torrent rushing across the road in front of me.

I had been watching for the main migration of elk for many weeks. I had not been alone in my vigil. Every morning during the migration season, from late October to mid-December, Bob Wood of Grand Teton National Park and James Yorgason of the Wyoming Game and Fish Department get in their official green trucks and drive slowly down the snow-packed highways of the Jackson area. They are members of a cooperative elk migration study. Sometime during the migration, the herds will cross highways and roads. From tracks left in the snow, biologists hope to gain additional knowledge of the elk's movement.

Several days before, I had taken the opportunity to ride with Bob Wood on one of his track-counting trips. Equipped with a four-wheel drive pickup, spotting scope,

note pad, broom and rake, we left the park headquarters at Moose and began the two to three-hour trip. Even though it was mid-November, there was little snow on the ground and virtually none on the highways. "This kind of weather makes for bad track counting," Bob said before we left. "Don't expect much."

As we drove very slowly, Bob peered ahead and to the sides. Just one mile out of Moose, we stopped. Opening his door and walking to the back of the truck for the broom and rake, Bob went to work. As I watched, he explained.

"Since there's so little snow, we won't find many elk tracks crossing the blacktop. However, when the elk walk through the snow on either side of the road, bits of dirt and small pebbles cling to their hooves and legs. It falls off when they hit the hard pavement. After the snow melts, the dirt and rocks remain. These little pieces of mud and stuff that I'm sweeping are from their hooves."

Sure enough, when I looked closely I saw a stretch of road splattered with dried mud and small rocks.

"Over here in the snow at the road's edge are some tracks. Looks like about ten head of elk crossed during the night," Bob said, raking the tracks and leaving the snow unblemished except for the lines made by the rake's teeth. "What I'm doing with the rake is erasing those tracks and leaving the snow fresh so if more elk come tonight, they'll leave their tracks and we can find them in the morning. This way, we know how many elk crossed the highway the previous night. Jim Yorgason does the same thing in a different area. I think he's up on

As long as they are able, elk will paw through the snow in search of grass. But deepening snows will eventually force them downward to winter ranges.

the Buffalo River and Togwotee Pass today.

"The elk that cross at this spot probably aren't migrating. There's a big group of them that hangs out on the ridges above here and then feed down during the evening. They cross this road back and forth all night long.

"Usually when the elk are really migrating, you know it. There aren't scattered tracks like this. Where migrating elk have passed, I've seen a swath of ground four or five feet wide where the snow was packed as hard as cement. Sometimes, if the ground's bare, I've seen the grass, dirt and willows so torn that it looked like a bulldozer had come through. When you see that, you know the elk are really coming down, really moving."

Climbing back into the truck, we continued down the road. Stopping occasionally to tally more tracks and rake them out, Bob would say, "That's made by a moose," or "Looks like half a dozen came through here," or "A loner."

The sight of a sparkling mountain stream and its crystal white banks is only a prelude to the next violent winter storm. But for now, all is peaceful.

As we drove, Bob explained to me some of the intricacies of elk migration.

"During the past ten years, the main migration of elk has peaked in mid-November, long about this time. The beginning of the elk movement depends upon the snow depth higher up. And that fluctuates year to year. Right now there isn't enough snow to force the elk down. They're still in the high country and might not come down until December this year. Just to give you an idea, on this same

stretch of road at this same time last year, I was making my count on a snowmobile.

"Normally the elk will start filtering down in October, after the rut starts winding down. We'll start finding mud flakes about then. In November, when the real winter storms begin, the main herds will pass through in a hurry. Last year we didn't see a track until early November. Then a storm came and overnight there were elk tracks everywhere. In four days the tracks were scarce again. Just like that, the elk

46

Amid winter's first major storm, a group of bulls that have banded together after the rut prepares to move to lower country. Bulls and cows often migrate in separate groups and spend the winter apart.

were down out of the mountains, through the park and onto the refuge.

"Generally elk will follow about the same routes year after year, even using the same trails. I can show you places up in the Buffalo Valley where there's a narrow spot, maybe only a couple of feet wide, where the elk have come down year after year. They'll jump fences in the same spot, too, again and again. One rancher around Jackson got so he'd go out every fall and take down the top rail on one of his pole fences because he got tired of the elk knocking it down and breaking it in the same spot every year. On the Snake River, I've seen many times where elk will swim across the same spot time and time again. Sometimes they'll wait for the ice to freeze solid in that spot so they can walk across. They won't go a hundred yards upriver or down to an unfrozen spot or even one that's shallower and less treacherous. That's where they've been crossing in the past, and that's where they'll continue to cross it. Sometimes that leads to problems. If the ice won't hold their weight and they are in a hurry, they'll go across anyway. The ice will break and they'll fall through. If they can't break the ice on into shore or turn around and swim back, they'll drown. If a lead animal falls through and others are following, sometimes the whole bunch is lost. Last fall, nine head died that way.

"Two years ago one of the rangers found three elk trapped by ice in the river. They couldn't go forward or turn around. He got a canoe and an axe and went upriver and floated down to them on a part of the river that wasn't frozen. When he got as close as he could, he began chopping. Those elk

followed him right out of there. When they got back up on shore there were several hunters waiting for the elk. They hadn't wanted to shoot them out in the water and take a chance on losing the meat. Besides, the river was off limits. They were just waiting until the elk got out. When the ranger saw them he told them to put the guns away, those elk were going on through. Not all the hunters are that way, but there's a few.

"The elk will cross rivers in the same spot when they leave the refuge and go north in the spring. When the cows have little ones with them, that can be a problem. The cows swim across and they forget that this is the first time for the babies. The little guys are unsure, scared and weak. Usually all the cows end up on one side of the river and all the calves on the other. There's a lot of squealing, bleating, whistling and other racket before the mess gets straightened out. The cows usually swim back across and coax their calves into the water. After a calf gets over the initial shock, he's a good little swimmer.

"Elk are strong travelers. In the past, as an experiment to see how strong the instinctive urge is to migrate to their home ranges, quite a few elk were trapped and tagged. One cow was taken from the elk nearly one hundred miles away and released. Six years later she was hit by a car on a highway right here in the park.

"The fellows that feed the elk every winter on the refuge get so they know a particular elk. Maybe he's got some distinctive feature that sets him apart from the rest of the elk. They'll tell you that the same elk will come back to the same feeding area winter after winter.

"Now we've got color-coded collars, even a few with small transmitters on them so that we can track an elk by radio and follow his every move. One of these days, all the pieces to the puzzle will fit together and we'll know a little about elk migration. Right now, we've just barely scratched the surface."

At noon, Bob and I arrived back at park headquarters. Bob had counted over thirty tracks. The elk were not moving. Like other biologists and game managers, he would continue to go out in the mornings. Waiting. Watching.

During the days following my visit with Bob Wood I, too, waited and watched. Each morning I posted myself in an area where I thought the elk might pass. There, crouching in the snow with my camera equipment, I would wait until the night's cold and darkness forced me to leave. After watching for six days, I happened to see the moving elk, and even that was an accident. I was driving home, returning from my waiting spot. Suddenly, just as I drove around a bend in the road my headlights picked up the reflections of the elks' eyes and the shadowy moving forms of their bodies. I sat watching the herds file across the road for many long hours that night. It was a sight I will never forget.

I am content to leave the statistics and calculations concerning elk migration to the biologists and game managers. To relegate their movement to mathematics is too impersonal for me. The movement of the Teton elk, to me, is one of wonder and mystery; an example of ancient forces at work in a modern world.

The elk's winter range is often shared by bighorn sheep, but the large number of elk often strip the land of grasses leaving little for other game. Bighorn sheep are one of the easiest of wild animals to win the confidence of and will eventually allow a person to approach them, although it may take many days of patient waiting.

One late afternoon, while I was photographing a group of wintering rams, a blizzard struck, erasing all landmarks and my sense of direction. With night approaching and the storm growing more intense, I walked in among the sheep. Turning into the storm, they eventually led me from the mountainside. Once out of the swirling snow, I recognized the trail back to camp, a welcome sight to be sure.

6. BLOODY NOVEMBER

It is mid-morning, November 15, 1974. The mountains are lost in clouds and it is snowing steadily. The flakes swirl through the air, landing lightly upon the ground to dissolve. For the past two hours a steady stream of cars has been moving up and down the blacktop that runs by the sagebrush flats and meadows of an area known as Mormon Row. Every now and then a vehicle—normally a pickup truck or jeep—stops, the window comes down and a pair of binoculars or a spotting scope pops out. Usually the vehicle moves on.

A jeep stops next to my truck. A man dressed in a red and black checkered coat and sporting an orange cap and a whiskered face sticks his head out the window. Beside him in the seat is a young boy and two rifles. The car tag is from California.

"Seen anything?" the man asks.

"No," I reply.

"Not enough snow," he says, grimacing. "Not enough to bring 'em down. We heard this morning that there's over 3,000 elk in Yellowstone Park and it didn't look like they were in any hurry to come down. If you ask me, it's a lousy goddamn year for hunting. Well, good luck."

The window is rolled up and the jeep roars off.

At dawn, November 27th, on a snowy, cold morning, four cows and three bull elk trot down out of the timbered mountain foothills and into Mormon Row. Even from a great distance, they are starkly visible on the flat, treeless plain. I see them only briefly. Before I can turn the ignition of my truck and drive closer, there is a distant crack, and then another. Suddenly the air is split with echoing, hollow roars and distant sounds like kernels of popcorn hitting a metal lid. One by one, as if in slow motion, the elk crumple and fall. Then the fields of Mormon Row are silent once again.

As I drive closer, I see that the seven elk have fallen less than one hundred yards from the blacktop road. Fifteen hunters walk toward them, yellow tags fluttering in their hands. Two pull a high-wheeled cart behind them. The bulls are tagged first. An argument ensues over one, the largest. The

Nothing had prepared me to watch the elk, which I had spent so much time studying and photographing, being shot down like so many sheep in a pen. I drove back to Jackson that morning feeling sick, empty and mad. I was determined to find out more about this hunt.

dispute is settled when one of the three arguing drops to his knees and begins gutting the elk. Reluctantly, the two other hunters tag cows, while still others shoulder their scope-sighted rifles, walk back to the cars, slam the doors and drive off.

These scenes have occurred in Grand Teton National Park every fall since 1950. The sportsmen who do the shooting are officially fulfilling a duty as "deputized wardens." Their targets are the large number of migrating elk that cross the flatlands enroute to the National Elk Refuge.

For many years before coming to Jackson, I had read stories about the firing lines on the sagebrush flats in Grand Teton Park and the elk slaughter that takes place there. The stories were always filled with statistics tabulating the kill. Somehow I felt prepared to see the real thing, but I was not. No amount of reading in a distant, well-heated room had prepared me for the signs with bold black lettering proclaiming "Hunting" and "No Hunting" that had been placed along the roads and in the scenic turnouts of the park. Or the sight of car after car filled with orange-capped hunters being driven up and down the roads of one of America's great wildlife sanctuaries. Or the hunting of supposedly "protected" animals that were far more accustomed to the click of a tourist's camera than the click of a rifle's safety being flipped from "on" to "off." Nothing I had read prepared me to watch the elk, which I had spent so much time studying and photographing, being shot down like so many sheep in a pen. After November 27th,

the stories I had read earlier seemed antiseptic. The statistics seemed vague and remote. I drove back to Jackson that morning feeling sick, empty and mad. I was determined to find out more about this hunt.

Probably no one has better expressed the philosophy behind the National Park System than Andrew Drury, a former director of the National Park Service, when he wrote in *National Parks Magazine* in 1949:

"No resources should be consumed or features destroyed through lumbering, grazing, mining, hunting, water control developments or other industrial uses.

"If we are going to succeed in preserving the greatness of the national parks, they must be held inviolate. They represent the last stand of primitive America. If we are going to whittle away at them we should recognize, at the very beginning, that all such whittlings are cumulative and that the end result will be mediocrity. Greatness will be gone."

It is ironic that in 1950, only one year after Mr. Drury's famous statement was published, the 81st Congress put its stamp of approval on Public Law 787, portions of which read:

"Section 6 (a). The Wyoming Game and Fish Commission and the National Park Service shall devise from technical information and other pertinent data assembled or produced by necessary field studies of investigation conducted jointly by the technical and administrative personnel of the agencies involved, and recommend to the Secretary of the Interior and the Governor of Wyoming for their joint approval a program to insure the permanent conservation of the elk within the Grand Teton National Park established by this act. *Such program shall include the controlled reduction of elk in such park by hunters licensed by the state of Wyoming and deputized as rangers by the Secretary of the Interior, when it is found necessary for the purpose of proper management and protection of the elk.*

"Section 6 (b) . . . controlled reduction shall apply only to the lands within the Park which lies east of the Snake River which lies north of the present boundaries of Grand Teton Park. . . ."

Public Law 787, with its carefully outlined program for controlled reduction and the resultant roadside hunting and killing of elk in Grand Teton Park, was not born out of anyone's intention to destroy the principles and ideals of the National Park Service. Nor was it some Congressman's whim to allow hunters to kill elk in a sacred place. Rather, the law was the result of a last drastic resort to offset the many things that had upset the natural balance between the elk of Jackson Hole and their environment.

In the 1800's there were probably more than 60,000 elk in the Jackson Hole region. These elk had a summer range in the surrounding mountains consisting of millions of acres. At one time, the elk had a large wintering area in the lower country around Jackson. Their population was kept in check by disease, starvation and predators such as grizzly bears, cougars and wolves. As recently as 1911, wolves killed an estimated 1,000 elk a year in Jackson Hole, according to early day biologist E. A. Preble. When the elk increased beyond

what their winter range could support and their predators could kill, the excess starved.

When settlement came, taking up much of the elk's winter range for livestock and crops, there was not enough grass left during the winter to support the large herds. Thousands starved. To make matters worse, the predators were killed off, sometimes for sport and bounty. On one hand, the elk could readily exist on the vast summer ranges, their ever-increasing

Cut off from the herd, its hindquarters raw from the slashing attacks of coyotes, this elk yearling awaits the final scene in the drama between predator and prey. Coyotes rarely attempt to kill full-grown elk, preferring instead very young calves and smaller game. But during winter, small game is hard to catch and the deep snow hinders and weakens the larger elk, making them susceptible.

numbers uncropped by predators. On the other hand, there were not enough of their ancient wintering grounds left to support them. By the 1920's the elk population, through hunting and starvation, had dwindled to near its present count of 20,000. To prevent further starvation, some 8,000 to 10,000 of these elk were fed hay during the winters on the 23,000 acre National Elk Refuge.

Today, the situation is basically the same. An average of about 8,000 elk are fed each winter on the refuge. About 3,000 of these elk summer on national forest land. They are allowed to be hunted each fall on the forest lands and their yearly increase kept in check in accordance with what the refuge can support. The remaining 5,000 elk summer in southern Yellowstone and northern Grand Teton Parks. These 5,000 park elk are within the protection of the national parks, however, and could not be hunted until recent years. Without predators and hunters these herds were free to increase their number.

Biologists estimate that the elk of Jackson Hole, unchecked by predation, increase their number by about 20 percent annually. If left alone, the park elk would soon increase by several thousands. These great numbers of elk, combined with those of the forest elk, would soon be more than what the refuge could support. Mass starvation would take place.

While starvation has been a part of the elks' natural life cycle for thousands of years, it is not probable that anyone would like to see hundreds of them die slowly within the confines of the refuge, especially since it was pity for the starving elk

that first prompted establishment of the winter feeding program. Before they died, the starving elk would probably eat the refuge's grasses and trees into the ground, thereby compounding the problem of an already critical shortage of natural browse.

To prevent such starvation, a way had to be found to control the large numbers of park elk. Allowing the elk to be hunted, although a weak substitute at best, seemed the only solution. The hunting, it was determined, would have to take place either on national park lands or on the refuge. A hunt on refuge lands, where the elk congregate in large herds for the winter, would result in a revolting slaughter, and it would endanger the people of Jackson since the refuge bordered the city. Also, if the hunt took place on the refuge, the elk might stop coming to the refuge altogether. The hunt, it was decided, would have to take place on national park lands and Public Law 787 was passed.

For many years, the number of elk to be killed by hunters on national park lands was estimated. To make matters simpler, however, an agreement was reached in 1975 between the National Elk Refuge and the Wyoming Game and Fish Commission, which has the responsibility of establishing the elk hunting seasons, issuing needed permits and deciding which lands will be open for hunting and for how long. Briefly, the agreement states that no more than 7,500 elk will be fed on the refuge in future winters.

Each winter, according to the agreement, refuge officials, biologists, and game managers will tally the elk wintering on the refuge. If, for example, they count 7,800 elk, they will then take into account an anticipated 20 percent increase to determine next year's potential herd. This example means that 1,860 elk—next year's increase of 1,560 elk plus the excess of 300 that already exists—would have to be eliminated the following winter to reduce the number of wintering elk to 7,500.

About 25 percent of the refuge elk come from the national forest lands where the forest elk are hunted and their yearly increase killed. The average number of forest elk that have been killed in past seasons, when subtracted from our example of 1,860 total elk to be cropped, leaves the number of park elk to be eliminated. A cold calculating method perhaps, but efficient.

The park elk have to be killed in the quickest, surest manner possible. The hunt has to be held in an area where there is the least amount of danger to park visitors, where the hunters can be controlled and where the elk will be relatively concentrated and easily found from year to year. The hunt must take place before the elk reach refuge lands, and as designated by law, it must happen only east of the Snake River, although other designated spots within the park are sometimes open for elk hunting.

Forced out of the high country by deepening winter snows, the park elk—the elk of the southern Yellowstone and northern Grand Teton Parks—somewhere along their migratory routes will cross a sagebrush flatland known as Antelope Flats and a grassy hay field known as Mormon Row. Although Antelope Flats was closed to hunting in 1974, both areas are within the boundaries of Grand Teton Park. This has

been the area designated for hunters and elk to meet. If everything works, the hunters will intercept the elk, the excess will be killed and everyone will be happy. Few times since its inception has the reduction program worked as successfully as it appears on paper. Human nature, the elk's wary instincts and unpredictable weather have created problems.

After ten years of being shot at, the elk have developed an understandable shyness toward humans and are wary of traveling through the sagebrush flatlands in broad daylight. Because of hunting pressures, the majority of fall migrations have started taking place at night. The elk pass through the flats under cover of darkness and arrive on the refuge unscathed and uncropped. By swimming the Snake River, many elk cross out of the hunting area. In the mornings, when the flats are empty and the hunters are driving up and down the roads, hundreds of elk may be seen just beyond the bold white signs which say: "No Hunting Beyond This Point. Grand Teton National Park."

Because of hunting, the elk are "spooky" year-round and run from the sight of a man although he may be hundreds of yards away. This makes it difficult, if not impossible, for tourists and others to photograph, study and observe the elk at close range. One park official assured me that it was "more natural" for the elk to react to men this way than the "unnatural" elk of central Yellowstone that have never been hunted and are quite tolerant of humans.

While the elk have developed a distrust of humans, other wildlife has not. Having never been hunted, these animals are quite

Hunters mill about on the road leading to the National Elk Refuge as they wait for the drawing that determines which of them are to be selected to hunt on refuge lands. To qualify for the refuge hunt, participants must also take a hunting safety course.

Numbered ticket stubs await to be drawn. Hunters holding coupons with matching numbers become eligible for the hunt.

tolerant of people, often allowing them to approach very close. For some of these animals, however, their first contact with the hunters is also their last. The combination of a few unsavory characters with guns, the frustration of a bad elk hunting season and the availability of numerous furred and feathered targets has led to poaching. In 1974 this was the list of animals and birds killed by poachers: a trumpeter swan (only recently removed from the endangered species list), several moose, two buffalo and thirty elk. The buffalo, although belonging to the park's herd of thirteen animals, had the misfortune of wandering across the boundary. Outside this invisible boundary the buffalo cannot be protected by national park laws. Neither are they classified as a game animal by the state of Wyoming and therefore cannot be protected by game laws. Seven of the elk were shot in one evening, the poacher disdainfully leaving his coffee cup in the field through which he drove to pick up the one elk he decided to keep. These are just the known kills. They do not include the park's smaller wildlife—the ravens, magpies, coyotes, etc.—that sometimes happen to wander into rifle range.

The punishment for shooting an animal, any animal, within the boundaries of a national park can result in confiscation of the person's vehicle, his weapons, and any equipment he might have used; revocation of his hunting license; a fine; and a jail sentence. Few poachers are caught, however. When they are, they are seldom given anything more than a small fine. It seems that the great wheels of justice do not really regard the illegal killing of a wild animal as much of a crime. As one member of the sheriff's department told me, "Christ, these guys come in here grinning, all covered with blood, pay their fines and walk back out. I even had a fella and his young son come in and the man said to me 'Even at that price it was worth it just to kill an elk'."

Because of increased poaching during the fall of 1974, a tougher stance was taken by the Game and Fish Department, the National Park Service and the Jackson Police. This crackdown included the closing of the park's inner road after sunset and the placing of a double shift of rangers on night duty. Hopefully, it won't be so easy for poachers to just walk out with their kill in the years to come.

Weather determines the success of the park hunt. More often than not, it is the reason the hunt is not successful. When the snow comes and drives the park elk out of the high country and toward the refuge, the elk may begin to move suddenly and be down on refuge lands in the course of several days. They are often through the hunting areas so fast that there is no time to act. By the time permits are issued and hunters deputized, most of the herds have made it intact to refuge lands. Often the elk movement occurs before the hunting season on park lands is opened in early November, or after it is closed.

The refuge has its own answer for early arrivals. A hunt is held on refuge lands, not so much for the kill, but to drive the elk back off refuge lands and into the laps of waiting hunters in the surrounding foothills. Years ago, this special hunt was open only to the elderly, crippled and young;

those who could not compete equally with healthier hunters in the field. But sportsmen of the world rose up in arms over this special treatment, calling it discrimination. So now the refuge hunt is open to anyone who can buy a tag and hold a rifle.

In 1974 the hunting season on national forest lands began on September 10. The park's hunt, where game managers hoped to intercept the park elk, started November 2. Usually park officials hope the annual increase of park elk will be killed sometime before the middle of November so they can pull down the hunting signs and allow Grand Teton to serve as a national park once again. It does not always work out. In early November, 1974, there was not enough snow to force the park elk to migrate, although the hunters had been issued permits, assigned areas and were eagerly waiting. By the middle of November there was still no snow and no elk had come. The season was extended a week. Finally, it was extended again into early December. In late December, long after the discouraged hunters had packed up and gone home, and the hunting signs had been stored away, the snow arrived and the park elk came down.

Every fall, hunters and guides mention that there seem to be fewer and fewer elk to hunt in the high country of the national forests. Yet the number of elk wintering on the refuge seems to remain large and stable. Why? There is a small segment of the Jackson herd that summers on the national forest land bordering Grand Teton and Yellowstone Parks. These unprotected forest elk, the smallest portion of the entire herd and those that could stand to be

"un-cropped" for several years, have been hunted nearly to annihilation in the hunters' zeal to get the park elk. They are hunted beginning September 10 on their own territory by hordes of hunters. When they come down out of the forest toward the refuge, they are caught by the hunters looking for park elk. There is no discernible difference between a national forest elk and a national park elk. To a hunter, an elk is an elk. If an elk is on park lands, then he is a park elk. If a forest elk makes it to the refuge early he is hunted there, or driven back onto the forest lands or park lands. So from opening day until the park closes its season, this small forest herd bears the lethal brunt of the reduction program. When the tally is made of the wintering population and the figures for the next year's kill established, these overly hunted forest elk will be counted in with the large numbers of park elk which have been safely multiplying in protection. The next fall the process will be repeated. In time, there may not be any elk on the lands of the national forest.

When the limit was set on the number of elk allowed to winter on refuge lands, the cropping process became the responsibility of the Wyoming Game and Fish Department. It is a game manager's nightmare.

When Congress allowed elk hunting to take place on the east side of the Snake River, it was thought that that would be sufficient. Game and Fish Department officials feel differently, however. They would like to see the west side of the river opened as well. This, they say, would avoid the firing line situation that occurs when the elk come through the narrow strip of territory east of the Snake River. Extending the hunt area would give hunters a hunt of a higher quality and take the killing away from the roads where it would be less obnoxious to visitors.

As one Game Department spokesman told me, "What's the difference? You're already hunting the east side. If we could hunt the whole park and put the number of hunters in there we wanted and set the season the length we needed it, we could take the pressure off the national forest elk which are cropped anyway, and take the increase of park elk perpetually every year. That's the beautiful thing about an elk herd, or any game herd. They are a renewable resource. You can take the increase every year and still end up with what you started out with originally.

"There is a lot of controversy over this hunt. 'Slaughter of Antelope Flats' it's called by a lot of people—hunters and non-hunters alike. There are a lot of organizations that would like to stop the hunting in Grand Teton and are putting the pressure on through Congress. But they are doing it to the detriment of the elk herd. A lot of people say, 'Gee, wouldn't it be nice if things were just left alone. Back to nature. Nature's way.' But they don't realize that nature's way became no more when the first white man settled in America. White men have disrupted the entire process and now, instead of predation and disease, you have the hunter. Unless you want a lot of starving elk, those elk have to be cropped. I've watched elk starve and it's not pleasant. If some of those people back east who are clamoring for an end to the hunting had to come out here and watch hundreds

of those elk starve to death, I'm sure they would have a change of mind.

"Teton Park has the most tightly controlled hunt I've ever seen or heard about. We issue about 2,500 permits for the park area and, historically, about half of these people show up for the hunt. Out of those that come to hunt, depending upon the snow and weather, we have about a 50 percent success ratio. That means we harvest about 500-800 head of elk. (The average annual kill from 1968-1974 was 579.) Now these elk cross erratically, in short bursts, and that's just about all the hunters we are going to be able to have out there and still have a safety factor. Most of the hunt occurs in the flat country where you can sit with a spotting scope and see everything that goes on. The cripple loss is much less than it would be in a national forest or wooded area. We have a minimum of three guys out there every morning and the park service has at least that many. If an elk gets crippled or wounded, one of us is going to kill it. You can't say that about any other kind of hunt.

"A lot of people in the excitement of the hunt don't realize they've killed an elk. Or maybe they've shot a cow and wanted a bull and won't claim it. Many times one of our people will have to say, 'Pardner, you got your elk, now get out there and get it.' You have to do that for safety's sake, and for the game's sake. You just can't let people go into this indiscriminately.

"Weather is the key in managing the Teton elk. If we could control the weather we could do exactly what we want with these elk. But every time we set a season we're gambling on the weather, making an

As the drawing for the hunt is taking place, these elk await the heavy snows that will force them down into the valley. Since being hunted, many elk now migrate at night.

educated guess and playing the odds. We have to guess as to when there will be enough snow to force the elk out of the park and then try to get the elk and the hunters to coincide. If we could get into that Yellowstone segment and let the rest go through we'd be tickled to death. But how do you do that? We could do it if we had an open-ended season. We could say, 'Okay, the season will begin when the game warden or the biologist says the Yellowstone elk are coming down.' But as yet we don't have the legal machinery to do that. Another problem is that people have to plan their vacations and days off and that might not coincide with when the elk are moving. So we just do the best we can.

"Nobody, ourselves included, likes the hunt that happens out there on the flats. But if anybody knows a better way to handle the situation please tell us."

As I found out, there is no definite right or wrong to the elk hunting in Grand Teton Park. There is no simple solution. The Teton elk exist as only a fraction of their former numbers. Their summer ranges are dissected by national park, national forest and private lands. The 23,000 acre refuge, their winter range, is a token portion of the vast area on which they must have once wintered. They no longer live within an ecosystem in which they can live and die naturally by predation, disease and starvation, unaffected by man as they once were for untold thousands of years. There can be no turning back of the clock. The Teton elk exist for man, whether for aesthetic or economic reasons, and their numbers have to be controlled by him, as distasteful as it might sometimes be.

7. HIGH COUNTRY MAGIC

At sunrise, final preparations had been made. Harold, John and Donald Turner, three guides, three horse wranglers, two cooks, nine hunters, myself and over seventy-five horses and mules began the first day of the hunt, an all-day ride to the main camp. Amid clouds of dry yellow dust churned by milling hooves, the sounds of nickering horses, braying mules, clanging bells, creaking leather and yelling men, the heavily loaded packstrings splashed across Pacific Creek and began climbing the trail toward the high country.

To me, there is no more beautiful country on earth than that of the high mountains surrounding Jackson Hole. It is a country of jagged mountain peaks whose rocky faces are often lost to clouds, a never-summer land of windswept timberlines, secluded basins and snaggletooth ridges that form the continent's spine. Here, melting snow waters give birth to rivers that flow to both oceans. Vast pine forests are dotted with stands of quaking aspen, lush grassy meadows, alpine lakes and clear, golden streams. This is a land of kaleidoscopic change. A bend in the trail, a change in the seasons, new wonders and new beauties continue to unfold. It is only fitting that this rugged land be inhabited by one of America's most magnificent of big game animals. This is elk country.

As we rode, I couldn't help but notice how deeply rutted and worn the trail was. Others had come this way; beaded, buckskinned Indians returning to their homelands with ponies laden with elk meat; trappers with ringing laughter and lonesome sounding harmonicas journeying over the mountains to a rendezvous; wealthy English sportsmen expending great quantities of wealth and ammunition; presidents such as Theodore Roosevelt, as well as naturalists like Ernest Thompson Seton and wildlife painters such as Carl Rungius. These mountains were hunting ground for all. And in the flickering of a campfire, the laughter inside a tent and the jingling of a packhorse's bell, their spirits still linger here, ghostly riders leading phantom packstrings toward the snow-whitened peaks.

Now, just as in decades past, the mountains of northwestern Wyoming harbor the largest concentration of huntable elk in North America. In search of his quarry, the guided hunter will be led into the most remote regions of the Tetons and, if successful, will return with pack mules laden with elk quarters. The majestic sights and sounds add to the magic that lures men into the high country.

Such trails serve, too, as a reminder of how plentiful the elk once were in this area. Here, a trapper named Osborne Russell wrote in his journal:

"August 28, 1839—I took a bath in the lake for probably half an hour and returned to camp about 4 p.m. Two of my comrades observed, 'Let us take a walk among the pines and kill an elk.'"

Forty years later an Englishman, William A. Baillie-Grohman, wrote:

"By the end of the second day in this natural game park . . . I killed nine bulls—all good heads—and without exaggeration could easily have trebled the number."

Now, just as in past decades, this country is still considered to have the finest elk hunting on the North American continent. Men still feel the lure of hunting in its mountains.

The Turners operate the Triangle X Dude Ranch in Jackson, Wyoming. During the summer, the Turners provide paying guests with wilderness pack trips, float trips down the Snake River, barbecues, square dances and a host of other activities. During the fall months, when the tourist season slackens, the Triangle X operates two elk hunting camps in the Teton Wilderness area adjacent to the southern boundary of Yellowstone Park. The elk hunting season in the Teton Wilderness begins September 10. It does not end until November, when the hunting season officially ends or heavy snows force the Turners to abandon the high country. During this short season the Turners attempt six to eight hunting trips every year. Each trip is ten days in duration. To get each group of hunters up into the mountains, find them an elk and bring them back down again within ten days, the brothers must work rapidly.

If the weather cooperates, enough snow falls to drive large numbers of elk out of their summer ranges in Yellowstone Park and into the Turners' hunting area. This affords quick kills and enough time between trips for the brothers to rest and relax. If the weather is hot and dry, the season becomes difficult and frustrating for guides and hunters alike. Such was the case when I packed with the Turners. There had been no snow. On the previous hunt only two elk had been killed. It had been the worst hunting season in the twenty-seven years that the Turners have outfitted and guided elk hunts.

On the morning that I packed with the Turners—the third hunt of the season—there was little hope of changing the run of bad weather. It was unseasonably warm. The sky was clear and bright. No storms were even hinted at in the weather forecast for the Pacific Northwest, storms that usually sweep down into Wyoming, filling the mountains with snow and forcing the elk to move.

The pack-trip hunt, Turner style, is the dream of nearly every red-blooded American hunter. For many men, such a hunt is a once-in-a-lifetime experience, the result of years of planning and saving.

Wyoming issues only 6,000 elk licenses a year to non-resident hunters who make up the bulk of the outfitters' clientele. In 1974, 9,000 non-residents applied for these 6,000 licenses. Since there are often more hunters than permits, hunters are matched with licenses through a drawing held by the Game and Fish Department in the early

During the fall of 1974, 47,420 elk hunters were issued licenses in the state of Wyoming and they killed 17,860 elk. Of these totals, 16,812 hunters hunted in the mountains surrounding Jackson Hole killing 3,777 elk. The Jackson kill was less than normal due to late snowfalls that did not drive the elk from protection of the national parks until after the hunting season. In a year with normal snowfall, an average of 4,500 elk are killed in the Jackson area.

There is no limit on the number of annual hunting licenses issued to Wyoming residents at a cost of $15.00 per license. The number of non-resident licenses issued each year is restricted to 6,000, however. In 1975 12,000 out-of-state hunters applied for the non-resident tags which cost $125.00 each.

spring prior to that year's hunting season.

Should a hunter be lucky in the drawing, his next consideration is to secure the services of a reputable guide. Good guides, such as the Turners, are often booked years in advance. The going rate for a pack horse hunt with the Turners is $100.00 a day, ten days minimum. Regardless of how early in the hunt he kills his elk, the hunter must still pay the outfitter the full ten-day fare, even if he is unsuccessful. Aside from the guide fee and the $125.00 cost of the license, the hunter must also supply his own clothing, personal gear, rifle, ammunition and travel expenses.

Until 1973 Wyoming hunting laws required that a non-resident hunter secure the use of a licensed guide. This was looked on by many as only a means of fleecing out-of-staters for as much money as possible. The law was taken to court and ruled unconstitutional and discriminatory. During the winter of 1974 the law was retried and partially reinstated. Now guides for non-resident hunters are once again required, but only on lands designated by the Forest Service as "wilderness areas." No motorized vehicles, equipment or permanent manmade structures are allowed in a wilderness area. There are four such areas in Wyoming, one of them being the Teton Wilderness in which the Turners hunt.

Basically the guide law is intended for the hunters' own good. Wyoming, especially the northwestern corner, is ruggedly foreboding country, awesome in size and as savage and quick to change in temperament as it is beautiful. For the novice elk hunter in poor physical condition and outfitted only with a map, compass and a sprinkling of survival knowledge, elk country, at its worst, can be a sure ticket to the obituary column.

Once the elk is killed, although no more than a mile or two from his vehicle or camp, the unguided hunter on foot has the imposing job of quartering and packing out the meat, head and horns. One hind quarter of a large bull weighs around 100 pounds. To carry these quarters one at a time on a packboard is a back-breaking task at best. In the high altitude where breathing comes hard, in the rough terrain where footing is often unsure and, frequently, in freezing rain or deep snow, this is not a feat easily performed by the average executive or even the construction worker. Yet every year there are articles in the leading hunting magazines advocating that hunters cut the cost of their elk hunt by "doing-it-themselves."

Compared to the alternatives, hunting with an experienced guide and outfitter at $100.00 a day is infinitely cheaper. The advantages of using professional services are overwhelming. Guides such as the Turners have been born and raised in the country they hunt. Hunters may depend on their knowledge, experience and equipment. They know in what areas elk are likely to be found and the shortcuts to get to them. They provide gentle horses with which the hunter and his guide can cover four times the distance in a day that a man hunting on foot can. They use a semi-permanent camp from which to hunt. The guide is experienced not only in finding elk, but in skinning, quartering and packing it back down on mules...an art in itself.

The Turners operate two hunting camps in the Teton Wilderness area located more than forty miles from the nearest paved highway. The Turners are among ninety outfitters operating hunting camps in the Jackson Hole area.

Elk hunting with guides and pack outfits was once for only the wealthy. Due to higher wages and increased leisure time, that condition no longer exists. Hunters now come from all walks of life.

The hunters I met and lived with during the ten days I spent in the Turners' hunting camp included a subway conductor, bricklayer, construction foreman, plumber, insurance agent, oral surgeon, real estate agent, college student and a retired butcher, aged seventy-nine. Of these nine men, three had hunted elk unsuccessfully with other outfitters in previous years and hoped for a change in luck. Three were newcomers to elk hunting and three had hunted with the Turners in years past and would continue to do so each year as long as their luck in drawing elk tags held out.

To an outfitter, repeat customers are like money in the bank. The ability to find elk and provide a good hunt and a friendly camp atmosphere will draw satisfied clients back year after year. They, in turn, will provide good word-of-mouth advertising.

"For the most part," Donald Turner said, "if we show a hunter a good hunt, he'll come back. By a good hunt I don't mean he necessarily has to kill an elk. We don't make any guarantees. On the last hunt when we only got two elk, most of those fellows really didn't care. They knew it was hot and dry and the hunting was bad. But they'd been with us before when it was real good.

"Most of our people have been coming with us for a number of years. On some of these hunts it's like a big family reunion. If we have hunted with a fellow and know him and he wants to come back, we'll

Harold is the oldest of the Turner brothers and, although the three share equally in running the camp, he is the recognized leader. During a typical season the brothers will employ three guides, three horse wranglers and two cooks.

In the evenings the horses and mules are let out to graze. Before dawn of the next morning, horse wranglers will round up the scattered bands with the aid of a few herd leaders wearing belled collars and bring them back to camp for selection by hunters and guides.

welcome him and try to find room. A lot of them do want to come back and I guess that's because we've got a good reputation. That reputation is the best advertising an outfitter's got."

The Turners' main hunting camp, the largest, is found in a broad meadow near the bubbling waters of a stream known as Mink Creek. The upper camp is some seven miles further upstream. John took two of the hunters, a cook and a horse wrangler with him to the upper camp. Harold and Donald stayed with the remaining seven hunters, the rest of the crew and myself at the lower camp.

By most standards, the Turners' set-up was elaborate. It consisted of eleven canvas tents: one large tent for cooking which includes a long table and folding chairs, two smaller tents for storing riding equipment and grain for the horses and mules, and eight sleeping tents complete with wood burning heaters, kerosene lanterns and log bunks covered with down-filled sleeping bags. There were two wooden corrals. There was even an outhouse. Located in a wilderness area, the camp was void of any motorized or mechanical sounds. Silence and the beautiful surroundings reigned supreme.

The first night, while sitting outside the cook tent with Harold, I had a chance to visit with him about the guide business. It was one of the few times during the ten days that I had a chance to talk with a relaxed Turner.

Harold Turner is a towering, raw-boned man with a sun-blackened face and a three-day-old beard. Almost traditionally, he wears a dirty, sweat-encrusted, brown

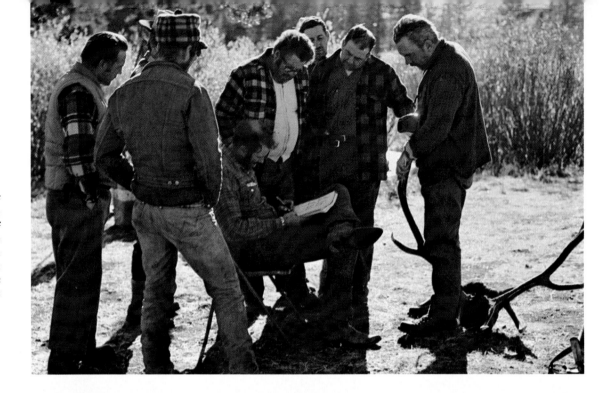

With hunters looking on, Harold Turner records the measurements of a rack of antlers to determine if it is worthy of the record book. One of the largest bull elk ever recorded was killed in the Jackson Hole area. The main beams of the huge elk were sixty-one and three quarters inches long, with eight points on one side and seven on the other.

Probably the hardest work to be done on an elk hunt is the skinning, quartering and packing of the meat. Mules are used to carry the quarters, not only because of their sure-footed ways, but because of their ability to carry heavy loads and their "good sense." When loading and unloading, leather blinders are used, for with mules "out of sight is out of mind."

Stetson that long ago lost any of its store-bought shape, a pair of faded saddleworn Levi's and a blue woolen shirt held together by numerous patches of varying sizes. In a small leather sheath on his belt was a folding knife with a four-inch blade.

Harold is an easy going man who smiles often and speaks with a slow northern drawl.

"You know, every year before the hunting season begins we come up here and build this camp. Since this is a wilderness area we can't use any motorized equipment like power saws. We have to go from the ground up with saws, axes, horses and muscle power. All the time we're putting it together, we know that on the last hunt of the season we're going to have to tear it all back down. Sometimes when I'm sawing up logs to be split into stove wood, or standing out there in a blizzard trying to pull a tent down with half-frozen fingers, I wish some of the people who enact some of that legislation would come up here and do a little of this. Then again, it's all for the good of the land. Just the sound of a power saw, even a long ways away, would sure wreck the silence. Today that kind of silence, the silence of the wilderness, is getting hard to find. After a few days up here you even start to cuss airplanes flying over.

"All of our hunters are up here to kill an elk. That's for sure. But you know, down deep most of them are up here to get away from the sounds and pressures of city life. An elk is kind of an excuse to do that.

"We try to give all our hunters a feeling for this country and the animals they are hunting. If we wanted, we could bring hunters up here for two days, five days or whatever and try to find them an elk. But that's cutting it close. Ten days is about right and usually after that long a time a hunter leaves with something more than dead meat.

"The guiding business is surrounded by a lot of Daniel Boone-type romanticism, being in the great out-of-doors, hunting and fishing, and the like. Somebody once said, 'Glamour tends to dissolve in sweat.' That sums up working as a hunting guide. Ninety percent of it is nothing more than hard work and and long hours. After you've watched several hundred elk get shot, skinned them, quartered them and lifted them aboard a pack mule, the romantic side of guiding wears pretty thin. It's not unusual for a guide to go sour after only a few seasons.

"And killing that elk is just part of the story, kind of like the portion of an iceberg sticking out of the water. The main part—the business part, the dealing with people, all kinds of people—is below the surface.

"If a guy isn't born into the guiding business it's hard to break in. Hard to get the capital for the investment in equipment. This camp represents many long years. It took us a long time to build it up to what we have today, and it takes a lot of time, money and work to keep it going."

Within the past few years a great many people have started to question the hunter, his motives and purpose, and the whole idea of hunting as a sport. Modern technology has taken the hunter far beyond being on equal terms with his quarry. Against scope-sighted, semi-automatic rifles, carefully engineered bullets, topographical maps, airplanes, spotting scopes

72

Part of the romance of a high country elk hunt is relaxing by the stove in the main cook tent after supper, playing poker and swapping yarns.

and thousands of other items designed to give the neophyte the greatest chance of securing his trophy, an animal such as an elk is hardly a match. The business of finding and killing has been reduced to its most convenient and simplest terms.

One cannot help but feel that in the case of the guided elk hunter this convenience has been taken even one step further. Little if any real knowledge of the elk, his habits and his environment, is required of the hunter. He does not have to find the animal, the guide does that. All the hunter has to do is pay his money, follow along, squeeze the trigger and kill his prey. The guide will skin it and pack it back down. Other than some hard breathing and a few saddle sores, the hunter does not suffer unduly for his trophy.

Perhaps as a result of our hurry-up, instant-everything society, a great majority of hunters prefer the hunt to be this way. The quicker and neater the package, the better.

Unscrupulous outfitters and guides promote a quick hunt. They want to get a client his elk and whisk him out to make room for another hunter. It's purely a matter of economics. In such cases, the enjoyment of the hunt, the pleasure of being afield and experiencing the wilderness is sadly forgotten or replaced with a single-minded lust to kill.

Every hunter has his own deep convictions and personal feelings about the hunting and killing of an elk. For some it may represent only a mounted head on the wall. To others, however, there is a certain undefinable magic in the name "elk" and the beautifully majestic mountain country

in which he lives. This is the same magic that has made the elk honored and loved by those who have hunted him through the centuries. Perhaps the magic of hunting this great deer is what men purchase with their license and guide fees. The killing of him is secondary.

One hunter who has hunted elk with the Turners for four consecutive years may have expressed the feelings of many hunters with a statement he made to me.

"I don't really know why I hunt. I just do. I enjoy it. Not the killing, that doesn't matter. I guess you really can't call it sporting for the elk. I mean after all, the odds are pretty much in our favor with guides and high-powered rifles.

"For a real hard hunt and matching of wits, I'll take a deer in a brush patch back home over an elk any old day. I sure don't come up here for the meat. For what I pay in one day here I could nearly buy a whole side of beef. Mostly, I like getting away. I can come up here once a year for ten days and forget about the suburbs and the office for a while."

During my ten days I found that "getting away" has a lot to do with why men hire guides and hunt elk. An elk is an excuse to be afield, away from the office and confines of city living. It's a chance to be rejuvenated and close to nature. For many hunters an elk hunt is their only chance to ever be in real wilderness. The pack trip hunt provides a storehouse of memories and experiences that could be received in no other way.

While following guide Donald Turner and his hunter George Foty, I began to see a little of the magic in elk hunting. The

feelings and mystique of the high country hunt began to creep into my blood.

Elk hunting is hearing the sound of the horses' bells long into the night and walking out under a night sky filled with thousands of stars whose brilliance is undimmed by city lights or smog. It is waking up in a cold tent, filling the stove with wood and waiting for it to hiss and roar to life. It is walking out of the cook tent in the mornings with a cup of hot coffee, watching morning's first light strike the highest mountain peaks and feeling the biting cold of the autumn air. It is leaving in the mornings, joints stiff and cold, and feeling the horse work as he goes up the trail. It is thinking, as you ride, that maybe today will be the day.

Elk hunting is seeing high wild places that few people ever see in the fall of the year when the aspens are shimmering golden. It is walking silently through dark, thick stands of timber, muscles knotted, nerves tense, heart throbbing, eyes straining. It is long hours of riding and speaking in whispers, then returning to camp long after dark, humped over with cold in the saddle, swaying to the horse's movement and finally, exhausted and nearly asleep, coming to a stop in front of the hunting camp which glows bright orange.

Elk hunting is seeing the first snow of the season and riding in it, cheeks and ears stinging with cold. It is seeing for the first time a grizzly bear's track in the snow—a track so big that the guide can fit his entire overshoe into it—and feeling the hairs on the back of your neck crawl with excitement. It is seeing a bald eagle soar overhead to sit in a tree and watch you pass. It is hearing a raven's hoarse croak and the lonely howling of a coyote at dawn. It is hearing the "skreaking" of trees in the wind and the wailing roar of a storm pounding against the tent. It is the companionship, talk and laughter after the day is done as you sit with a glass of brandy in a warm tent.

Elk hunting is that one fluttering heartbeat when, after all the struggle and waiting, you approach a bull laying on the ground. It is realizing your own mortality in his death. It is standing over him with the rifle in your hands and feeling sorry that his life ended. In your mind you see him as he came out of the shadows and stood, the last rays of daylight tipping his coat golden. Perhaps if it were within your power you would bring him back to life so that he might go royally, majestically on his way. Perhaps you touch his antlers and feel the roughness of the beams and smoothness of the points and wonder at the places he has been and the sights he has seen. It is knowing that for you the hunt is over. The moment the trigger was pulled, the hunt, the expectation and the thrills were over. Tomorrow, with the guide and pack mules, you will bring the elk down, skinned and quartered, his antlers sawed off, his living image reduced to a memory that will never fade. This perhaps is the magic men seek in a high country elk hunt.

After the hunt with the Turners had ended, the nine hunters and myself were taken back down country. The snow had come. The hunters had each killed an elk. The next morning, Harold, John and Donald would again leave with ten new hunters for ten more days.

Wrapped in cheese cloth for protection from debris and insects, elk quarters are hung by wire from a pole. One night during the hunt a grizzly bear strolled into camp and carted one of the 100-pound quarters away, leaving only his tracks and a dangling piece of wire as evidence of his theft.

8. WINTER SAGA

Snow never leaves the Teton country. Even during the summer it may be seen, a distant glimmering whiteness on the high mountains. There, a constant reminder of winter past, it waits patiently for its season to come once again.

In October, the storms begin. Gray clouds boil forebodingly on the horizon for days and then suddenly, as if released by a wrathful god, roar down upon the landscape. The storms last for days, sometimes weeks, halt and then resume once more as if engaged in a furious battle to smother the land with snow.

In the storms' aftermath, beneath the soft contours of the snow and intricate patterns of ice, the familiar has become unrecognizable; the commonplace, magnificent. Whitened mountain peaks loom upward, their jagged edges sharply silhouetted against cloudless sapphire skies. The air, crisp with cold, shimmers with tiny ice crystals. Pine forests, boughs heavily laden with snow, stand like great, silent cathedrals. Waterfalls glisten, their roar muted beneath towering sheaths of ice.

In winter's beauty, wildlife wages a desperate, silent struggle for survival. Those species that can escape have flown south to warmer climates, burrowed into the ground to sleep or retired to dens to wait out the long winter months. Man has provided some measure of escape for the Teton elk. He has set aside some 23,000 acres of their ancient winter range to be saved from civilization's progress. He has fenced it from the highways and called it a refuge. Here, forced out of their summer ranges by deepening snows, thousands of elk spend the winter after a long, hazardous migration. The elk are within sight of a large motel, several housing additions and an elementary school. They are exhibited hourly to tourists who ride in horse drawn sleighs. They are trapped, transplanted and studied for disease.

Although the meshwire fences prevent elk and tourists' cars from colliding, their thin strands do not stop the whining ground blizzards or the sub-zero cold of winter. However, the fence provides a haven from winter in another way. Within

The beauty of winter often disguises the hardship it imposes on wildlife.

its confines, few elk starve to death. They are sustained by hay, and more recently, alfalfa pellets.

Through the winter, although I loved these elk, I grew to resent seeing them on the refuge. They reminded me of domestic cattle being pampered in a feedlot. As winter progressed, my visits to the refuge became less frequent and finally stopped altogether. Man's presence and his subsidy, although necessary, was all too obvious; his purpose too commercially foreboding. Preferring the silence of my touring skis and snowshoes to the noise of the sleigh, I began searching out other elk, those for whom winter still plays a vital role.

Such elk were not hard to find, at least not as difficult as one might imagine. Not all elk in Jackson Hole winter on the refuge. In fact, only 30 percent of the elk in this region can be found within the fences. Another 50 or 60 percent are fed hay on scattered feedgrounds by the Game and Fish Department. And what of the remaining small percentage for whom there will be no handouts? For these elk, like the deer, moose, bison, bighorn sheep and a score of others, there is no escape. They congregate alone or in small herds in the valleys and basins, along the rivers and on the wind-blown hillsides of the lower country. There they face snow which buries the grasses, freezing temperatures which maim and kill, slow starvation and endless hours of waiting. This is the story of one such elk.

The gray-horned bull was one of the many loners who, in addition to small groups of other elk, wintered in the mountains. I saw him often, standing on a lonely hillside, the wind curling plumes of snow around his legs and tossing the long dark hairs of his mane.

I frequently wondered what made him, and those like him, so boldly independent of the refuge and feedgrounds that thousands of his species had accepted. Perhaps he had fallen by the wayside during the downward migration and was caught by the storms which brought the deep snows. Perhaps the old bull knew that in the fall there were hunters seeking the massive antlers growing like weathered tree branches on his head, and he had remained hidden in his secret places until too late. Maybe he simply preferred the company of his own regal presence. Perhaps he distrusted men, all men, although they might feed him.

Through the winter I grew to admire the bull and even started making the mile-long trip on snowshoes once a week just to sit and watch him. In time, he grew to tolerate my presence and would lay, chewing his cud, silently contemplating me.

Then the storm came. It raged for a week with the ferocity that only a mountain storm in March can have. After the skies cleared, the temperature plummeted to far below zero and remained there day after day. When I again ventured out to see how the bull was doing, there was three feet of new snow on the ground. The hillside was barren of grass and the bull was nowhere in sight. Only his tracks, great plunging black holes punched in the frozen snow, remained. The edges of the tracks were flecked with blood and hair where the crust with its thousands of minute, razor sharp teeth had torn at the bull's legs as he lunged through the snow and ice. Several times as I

followed his trail, I found where the exhausted bull had lain down to rest. But always the tracks continued, a weaving, staggering line that meandered aimlessly across the windswept flats.

I found the bull in a small grove of aspen trees. Lifting his head, he eyed me drearily from his niche in the snow. His ribs were boldly outlined as if his hide had dried and shrunken to his frame. His sides rose and fell heavily with labored breathing. His proud neck was bent. His head tottered from side to side from the weight of his antlers. There was flesh exposed where the hair on one side of his face and along his back had fallen out with scabies. Exposed to such extreme cold the flesh looked like over-cooked meat that was on the verge of burning. Legs once powerfully muscular were thin with bones protruding and hair bloody and matted from pawing the snow in search of grass. The voice that had once sent deep roaring screams over the high meadows was now a raspy, wheezing cough.

Sitting on my snowshoes I envisioned the bull as he had been during the summer and fall months. Autumns ago he had probably been a powerful harem master. Time had taken its toll. Exhausted by long hours of defending his cows against rival bulls, his energies depleted from lack of feed, he had been robbed of his cows one by one until at last he was alone. In October, when I had first seen him, I made note of his antlers which, although massive and symmetrical, never turned darker than gray. Even then the bull had been by himself, wandering from meadow to meadow.

During the rut and winter I saw many such bulls. Old and exhausted, they could no longer hold their own against the competition of younger bulls and would breed no more cows. Their usefulness to the species gone, these old bulls drifted away to live a solitary existence. Resting, feeding and thinking the thoughts that old bulls must think, are all that filled the days.

Nature tolerates neither the unproductive nor the extraneous. The bulls would die. Eventually starvation, predators, disease or exposure to the winter would overtake them. None would succumb to old age.

Many times I had listened to and recorded the gray-horned bull's powerful bugle. I had watched through my camera's viewfinder as his hooves and antlers dug at the frosty grasses. Once, when I had ventured too close, he turned on me with a lowered, threatening head and scattered my camera equipment and courage in the dense thickets.

The fall months, with their lush grasses, seemed remote now. I sat, throat welling up, knowing that the gray-horned bull had seen his last winter. He would never rise from this spot again.

In his death the cycle would go on. The old bull would return to the earth and the grasses that had given him life and nourishment. He would enrich and fertilize the land for others. Young bulls, those he had driven away and beaten down, would step up through the bachelor ranks to take his place. Coyotes, magpies and bears would eat his flesh and scatter his bones. Rodents would chew them for the calcium they contained. The fragments of his bones would be washed down to the

Loners, such as this cow elk and the moose at far left, are found in all species of wildlife and during winter share the same struggle for survival.

rivers by the meltwater. Dissolved, they would eventually find the sea.

But the spirit and heritage of the old bull would remain forever here in the mountains. Somewhere, wintering in the lower country, there were cows, their flanks bulging with his calves. Young bulls with antlers that would grow large and massive, and perhaps have even a tint of gray in them, had been sired by the old bull during his brief reign as monarch. These products of the bull's seed would survive. They would return with the melting snow to the summer ranges. To these, the survivors, the winter would bring life. The melting snow water would feed and nourish the meadow grasses and fill the streams and lakes on which life depends. Because of snow, there would be abundance and plenty for all. On the summer ranges between the waning of one snow season and the beginning of another, winter would be forgotten. The business of life would go on. The gray-horned bull's descendants would reproduce, raise the young, renourish and refill, and prepare for winter once again. Yes, the cycle would go on. Truly, the gray-horned bull had left his legacy.

9. WINTERING WITH THE BIG HERD

During the winter, horse drawn sleighs take visitors to the National Elk Refuge to see the elk. Since walking on refuge lands is strictly prohibited and travel by vehicle is limited to a few snow-covered gravel roads, the sleigh is the only way to get a close look at what is called "the world's largest elk herd."

The first time I paid a dollar for a seat on one of the wooden benches, the sleigh was filled with thirteen other people, most of them skiers who had had enough of the slopes for one day. It was snowing. Larry Moore, the sleigh's driver, explained the ride rules: no getting off, no loud noises or movement. He then clucked to his team of Belgian horses and shook the reins. Manes encrusted with snow and coats steaming, the horses strained against their harness collars and dug their large hooves into the snow. For a moment, the sleigh creaked and groaned. Then, with a sharp crack, the sleigh lurched forward, its runners breaking free of the frozen ground. We were on our way.

At first the landscape was a barren white,

Hundreds of wintering elk stream past the camera's eye on the National Elk Refuge. The refuge and the surrounding mountains comprise their final stronghold against the onslaught of civilization.

In the evenings the elk often disperse, leaving the central portions of the refuge to move up into the foothills. There, during the night, they paw through the snow for grass. By daybreak they return to the lower country.

devoid of elk and any sound or movement other than our own. Then, suddenly, as if the snow had parted its white curtain, we sighted the herd. The elk were directly in front of us, a sea of brown that seemed to stretch to the horizon.

As we moved closer to the herd, two cows walked in front of the horses and stopped to one side. With their noses upthrust in a disdainful manner as if resentful of our intrusion, they watched us glide past. Cameras in mittened hands clicked and whirred. Then, we did the unbelievable, or so it seemed to me. We drove through the herd. The sea of brown elk parted to let us pass and flowed by on both sides of the sleigh almost close enough to touch. All around us were thousands of milling, feeding, sleeping elk. A few wheeled, their hooves sending up puffs of snow, and trotted away. Most did little more than twitch an ear or blink a sleepy eye in our presence.

Ever since the old man told me about counting three hundred elk in one herd, I had tried to imagine seeing that many elk. It was impossible to envision. Yet on that December day I stood looking out over thousands upon thousands of elk. The sight was overwhelming and I felt almost as if I had taken a step backward into America's past.

When more and more people tucked their cameras away and statements of "I'm cold" became more frequent than questions, Larry wheeled his team around and started back to the concession stand. Those large herds of elk were one of the most awesome and beautiful sights I had ever seen. I could not get enough of seeing them

and rode the sleigh three more times that day.

When I returned the next spring for my year of observing the elk, it was with the intention of finding out as much as I could about the winter home of the Teton elk, the National Elk Refuge.

The thousands of elk that winter upon the National Elk Refuge are known all over the continent as the "largest elk herd in the world," the "Jackson herd," or the "Southern Yellowstone herd." In truth, these great numbers of elk are not one single herd but the combination of many herds, large and small. They have been lumped under one heading simply for convenience. The elk winter in such massive concentrations because their modern winter range is severely limited in size. It is here in this relatively small area that they are fed by man so they can survive the winter. It has not always been so, however.

Elk have always wintered in Jackson Hole. But, depending on the elk's population, the severity of the winter and the amount of winter forage available, herds also migrated around or through Jackson to winter elsewhere. This I verified by talking with Jackson resident, Almar Nelson. Mr. Nelson has lived in Jackson since 1902. After serving in World War I, he became one of the first managers of the then newly established National Elk Refuge. He served in that capacity for thirty years. One morning, in the summer of 1974, I visited with Mr. Nelson about the elk migration out of Jackson.

"I can still remember the large herds of elk that would come down past our house," Mr. Nelson said. "I suppose they were

The elk that did winter in Jackson became the last of the great herds left in North America. Because of Jackson's remoteness they would be the last elk on earth to truly feel the pressures of civilization.

By 1890 permanent settlers had begun coming to the beautiful valley beneath the Tetons. The elk's predators were not compatible with the raising of livestock and the safety of the town's growing populace. By the early 1900's a full scale war on predators had begun. Within the span of a few years, most had been virtually exterminated or driven to the most remote portions of the mountains.

In 1907 lands east of the Snake River and south of Yellowstone Park's southern boundary were designated as the Teton Game Preserve in which hunting was not allowed. Intended to give the elk a hunting-free passage from Yellowstone Park to Jackson Hole, the formation of this preserve eliminated for 28 years one of the most popular elk hunting areas on the continent.

Because of fewer natural predators and since they were protected from hunting on the higher ranges, the elk herds grew larger and larger. At the same time, the elk's winter range in the valley was being consumed by an increasing number of homesteaders and ranchers. Progressively each winter, as the herds migrated down into Jackson, they found less land on which to winter and less forage to eat. Just prior to World War I, the herd had swollen to some 40,000 animals and there had been a great influx of settlers in Jackson Hole. The situation had reached climactic propor-

tions. Something would have to give.

During the winter of 1909, caught between snow-locked mountains and a barren winter range, the elk stripped the valley locust-like of all above-snow vegetation and even grew desperate enough to invade ranchers' haystacks. To keep the elk away from their precious hay, people often slept in the haystacks at night. More than a few ranchers sympathized with the starving elk and fed them along with their cattle. Taking the matter of saving the elk into their own hands, the people of Jackson raised $1,000.00 to purchase hay for feeding the elk. It would not be enough.

When spring came, there were some 2,000 dead elk on the valley's floor and ridge. The air was rancid with the stench of rotting carcasses. A Jackson rancher wrote of that winter:

"I have walked for a mile on dead elk . . . they would be dead usually along a steep hillside where the snow had blown off, and where they had been trying to get what little feed there was in sight. I know a rancher who pulled 450 dead elk out of his hay corral."

Another added:

"The heavy losses are in the calves. The mothers wean them in the month of January and if there isn't feed the little fellows soon get weak and die. It is pitiful to see the little fellows trying to make a living of it. They are so weak when they start to move they will fall down. The mothers paw in the snow and when they have gotten the snow pawed away there is nothing but bare ground in sight. They are so weak they can hardly travel and if they come to a fence, in trying to jump it they fall and are often

found in the wire tangled up and dead.''

Conditions worsened as the winter was followed by an unusual drought. Even the elks' summer range was barren. In anticipation of another disaster, the Wyoming legislature raised $5,000.00 and purchased hay. But before the winter storms of 1910 even began, great numbers of elk came down and were fed all that had been bought. There would be no more hay that winter. When the spring of 1911 came the herd numbered less than 20,000 animals. Winter had taken its toll.

Decimation of the herd also took place at the hands of tuskers. Each elk has two tusks called ''ivory'' growing on the upper jaw. Tusks of a mature bull are about the diameter of a person's thumb and three-fourths inch long. Before the coming of the white man's trade goods, Indians prized the tusks for decorative beauty. While visiting a western tribe in the 1800's, John James Audubon was presented a robe decorated with the ivories of fifty-six elk. The robe was valued at thirty horses, a horse being the Indian's most valuable possession. In the 1900's white men sought the tusks for members of the fraternal organization known as the ''Elks.'' Members would pay ten to twenty dollars for the ivories. An exceptional pair might bring eighty-five dollars. Hundreds of elk were killed only for their tusks. The carcasses were left to rot.

Working outside the law, many tuskers strapped elk hooves to the bottom of their boots, leaving no boot prints for wardens to follow. Few tuskers were caught and fewer were convicted.

Spearheading the drive to save the elk was Stephin N. Leek, an early day Jackson rancher and pioneer wildlife photographer. Leek spent much of his own time and money traveling throughout the United States presenting his photographs and lecturing on the problem of the Wyoming elk to any audience that would listen. Through Leek's writings, the starving elk and the tusker came to national attention. It was not long before the whole nation pleaded the cause of the great forest monarchs.

The Wyoming legislature took up the matter of the starving elk with the federal government and requested that Congress appropriate funds to buy lands for the creation of an elk winter refuge. In the spring of 1910 Edward Preble, a biologist from Washington, D. C., was detailed to Jackson to make a preliminary investigation of the situation. With the aid of D. C. Nowlin, who was state game warden at the time, Preble spent the entire spring, summer and fall months studying the elk problem.

In 1911, as a result of these investigations, Congress appropriated $20,000.00 toward hay purchases. The following year a refuge project was initiated in which Congress appropriated money to buy 1,760 acres along Flat Creek north of Jackson. This was joined with 1,040 acres of unentered public lands. On August 10, 1912, the National Elk Refuge was established for the care and preservation of the elk wintering in Jackson Hole.

The Isaac Walton League became interested in the elk refuge project and through public subscription raised enough money to purchase about 1,600 additional acres. Two years later these lands were deeded to

Staff members of the National Elk Refuge and the Wyoming Game and Fish Department periodically pen some of the elk in chutes to sample the herd for disease.

His antlers broken and entangled with barbed wire, the plight of the young bull at left exemplifies the elk's conflict with civilization. During the rut, a bull will often mistake a fence post for a sapling and rub his antlers against it. If he becomes entangled, the bull risks slow strangulation or catching the wire in brush and dying of starvation before he can work free. If he's fortunate, he'll survive until spring when the antlers are shed and with them, the troublesome wire.

Thousands of elk rush to eat the pellets dropped from the feed truck. One truck and driver can feed the entire refuge herd in about half a day.

the federal government and made a part of the elk refuge. In 1933 Congress appropriated five million dollars to be used for the purchase of marsh lands all over the United States for waterfowl sanctuaries. This fund was also to be used to enlarge the elk refuge. From those funds and through additional government land purchases and personal donations of both land and money, the refuge has grown to its present size of 23,754 acres.

Although existing primarily for the elk, the refuge also benefits other wildlife. There are a number of moose, mule deer, bighorn sheep and coyotes, as well as a small resident flock of rare trumpeter swans, wintering on refuge lands.

In past years as few as 5,000 or as many as 10,000 elk, depending on the depth of snow in the surrounding mountains, have wintered on refuge lands. The average is usually about 8,000 animals. Severe winter storms and freezing spring rains often make it impossible for the elk to paw through the snow for grass. When this happens they are fed hay. Ten tons of baled hay will feed the herd for about a week. Responsibility for feeding the elk belongs to Don Redfearn, refuge manager, and his small staff of people who work for the Department of the Interior's Bureau of Sport Fisheries and Wildlife.

Mr. Redfearn has been manager of the refuge since 1966. During an afternoon visit he told me:

"A lot of people have the idea that the refuge is a feeding ground, sort of an elk welfare program. That's not the image we'd like to convey at all, but it is the image the refuge presented not too long ago. We try to use the best of the refuge's natural resources and only supplement artificial food when it's really needed. In fact, there have been seven winters when the elk didn't have to be fed at all."

The hay for feeding the elk used to be raised in a co-operative effort by the National Park Service, the Wyoming Game and Fish Department and the National Elk Refuge. The Park Service provided the land on which to raise the hay, the Elk Refuge supplied the irrigation and farming and the Game and Fish Department handled the cutting and hauling of the hay. When the twenty-year agreement ended in 1972, the Park Service, in accordance with its policies to limit man-made development and commercial uses of the park, did not renew the agreement.

In anticipation of this, the Refuge had been experimenting with a new food to replace the hay, alfalfa pellets. Through the use of these pellets, Redfearn hopes not only to have a substitute for hay, but to improve the health and vitality of the herd, reduce labor costs and save time. He told me, "It used to take six men working in three two-man teams from 8 a.m. to 4:30 p.m. to feed the entire herd. They used horse drawn sleds. Now, one man can drive the pellet truck, feed the entire herd and reload for the next day and be finished by early afternoon."

Acting as a sort of pied piper, the specially built, 6-wheel drive feed truck can lead elk to different areas of the refuge, thus breaking up the large congregations and making the elk utilize more of the refuge's natural forage. By dispersing the large groups and taking them to cleaner feeding areas, the elk become less susceptible to communicable diseases.

The man responsible for much of the research and testing of the new pellets is Russell L. "Buzz" Robbins, a biologist for the U. S. Fish and Wildlife Services Research Center in Denver, Colorado. Working on the refuge since 1971, Robbins found in his studies of penned elk over a period of three winters that the elk fared better on pellets than hay. They came out of the winter with a more stable weight and in better health than those that had been fed hay. The elk tended to eat more of the pellets, wasting less and thus making them more economical. In one study, 24 percent of the hay fed was left uneaten. With pellets this loss was only 4 percent.

"Someday," Buzz told me, "once we learn what the elks' nutritional requirements are, we can add the necessary nutrients and vitamins to the pellets right at the mill. In the future we can even add antibiotics."

While on refuge lands some of the elk succumb to the rigors of winter. Many of these elk have been wounded or crippled during the hunting season. Others die of diseases, the most prevalent being scabies, a disease which causes their hair to fall out. In 1973, a hard winter, about 125 elk died. In 1974, a mild winter, only 18 died. The average amount of winter kill is only about 1 percent, which is quite a high success ratio and one of which many livestock ranchers would be proud. This winter loss is quickly taken care of by the large population of coyotes which act as the refuge's scavengers.

Things do not always go as smoothly on the elk refuge as they appear. From its beginnings, the feeding of the elk has been controversial. In 1909, the state game warden, D. C. Nowlin, wrote:

"If our elk are to remain really wild and to be hunted under restrictions as wild game, they should not be semi-domesticated and attracted to the ranches by continu-

Specially milled alfalfa pellets have replaced hay as feed for the wintering elk. Refuge tests show that the pellets, which are about two inches long, sustain the elk better than the hay.

92

A young cow penned in the chutes awaits her turn for checks of blood sample, weight and general health.

Perhaps the disease most common to elk is scabies which usually affects older bulls, causing their hair to fall out. During the extreme cold of winter, the loss of hair can be fatal. As yet, no one has determined the cause of scabies or a means of combating it.

ous winter feeding. Such treatment would soon take them out of the category of wild animals and put them in a class with the elk of eastern game parks."

Today, the controversy continues. Many people believe that the feeding should stop and the elk be returned to a natural balance with their environment. Under such conditions many elk would starve. The elk population would settle down to around 5,000 animals, a number that the winter range could support without man's help. In such a natural condition the hunting in Grand Teton Park to crop the excess could be eliminated, as well as the feeding program and all the expense that goes with it. This all sounds well and good. However, to advocate such a drastic change is to ignore several very relevant issues.

One reason the elk will never be returned to such a natural situation is simply because the vast majority of the public would never allow it. People are too willing to see nature through rose-colored glasses. They would never accept the predation and starvation that would have to occur for the herd to once again be in harmony with its winter grasses. Secondly, the elk are too valuable commercially to just let hundreds of them starve. Perhaps I should explain further.

Not too long ago a busload of visitors going through Yellowstone Park watched a bear kill an elk calf. This was a natural act of predation which occurs often in the wild, but usually not in the public eye. The effect of seeing this made most of those people on the bus violently ill. For many, it ruined the entire trip through the park. People cannot accept predation as a fact of

life. Not the predation that seems to occur just off screen in wildlife movies, not the predation that is read about in vague terms in books and articles, but real predation. The gut-wrenching emotions one feels when watching a pack of coyotes eat a yearling elk alive, or seeing a grizzly run down a winter-weakened bull and smash him to the ground, are not pleasant. Yet, they are the essence of life in this mountain land. They are realities that one must expect and accept as part of the natural scheme. But too many people have forgotten that the elk in his natural role is killed and eaten by predators. Instead of acceptance, the predator is abhorred and condemned. His quarry, the elk, is pitied, however.

Few tears were shed in Jackson Hole when the wolves were eliminated and the elk left free to propagate. But, when elk began starving because of their excess numbers the public found this distasteful, too, and clamored for the creation of a refuge on which to feed the elk. The lesson has not been learned yet. During the spring of 1975 when elk began starving to death along the highways of Yellowstone Park, national newspapers, magazines and television specials were filled with stories about the poor starving elk. The National Park Service was strongly criticized for standing by its policies of maintaining a natural situation and not feeding the elk hay. Throughout the situation, I did not hear any television commentator, radio announcer or newspaper writer mention that the elk of Yellowstone had been building up to an unnaturally high population peak for many years; that it is natural for elk to starve during the winter under wild conditions; that such starvation has been occurring for thousands of years; and that the purpose of a national park is to preserve an area and keep its ancient forces, even starvation, intact and free from mankind's sincere, but bungling hand. No one mentioned that the elk would return to their summer ranges in fewer numbers; that the overgrazed grasses would return; and that the elk would once again be in harmony with their environment.

It was this same kind of misunderstanding and pity for the elk, along with his taking of the elk's natural wintering areas, that led man to create the elk refuge and its feeding program. It is for that reason, too, that the feeding will not stop. Most people are all for a natural situation as long as they are not really confronted with it. Watching hundreds of elk starve to death to arrive at a balance between their numbers and the refuge lands would more than likely turn the stomach of the most ardent "stop the feeding" advocate.

Placing the elk on a more natural basis would also deny many people of Jackson their livelihoods. There is a price attached to each elk in the form of revenue from hunters in the fall and tourists in the summer. These people come to Jackson and expect to see or kill elk. And they pay for it, boosting the local economy by millions of dollars. Hunting outfitters, merchants, gas station owners, auto repairmen, sporting goods stores . . . all make money either directly or indirectly from the elk. To suddenly eliminate a large portion of these elk might cause a minor depression in Jackson Hole. The elk in Jackson exist for

Antlers gathered from the National Elk Refuge are auctioned every spring in the town square of Jackson for the benefit of the local Boy Scouts. The antlers are wired together in bundles and sold to the highest bidder. Left to the elements, the antlers would soon disintegrate and fertilize the soil.

man's pleasure and economic benefit. Right now they are just too valuable a commodity not to preserve by winter feeding.

While still on refuge lands the bulls shed their antlers. During the spring the fallen antlers are collected under a refuge special use permit by the local Scout troop. They are then sold at a fund-raising auction the first Saturday in May in the town square. The antlers are sold by the pound. Most are bought by oriental buyers who take them back to their homelands and grind them up. This powder is then sold as a love potion throughout the Far East, and is also used in the manufacturing of certain vitamins.

In 1973, when the oriental buyers were bidding against each other, the Scouts raised a whopping $19,000.00. In 1974, however, the bidders got together beforehand and decided on the top price they would pay. This netted the Scouts only $5,805.00. At any rate, the Jackson Hole Scout troop must surely be the richest in the nation.

In years past, the antler auction was considered a part of Jackson's local color. Now, more than a few citizens look upon it differently. As one resident told me, "The antlers should be left on the ground to return to the soil as fertilizer. After all that's what they do naturally. The antlers are picked up on federal land that all of us pay for with taxes. They are the property of the whole nation. Not just the local Boy Scouts.

"If the antlers are used at all it should be to help defray the cost of feeding the elk. As far as I'm concerned the auction is just a money

thing like everything else with this elk herd."

A resident supporting the auction told me, "Well, the antlers are just going to disintegrate and they might just as well be used by somebody for something. Why not the Scouts?"

That statement just about sums up the interaction between man and elk in Jackson Hole. The elk are always going to be used by somebody for something. As long as they are valued as a means of making money then there is no doubt that they will be fed and preserved as the largest herd of elk in the world. If they ever lose that value it is doubtful that they will be around in great numbers much longer. Few people save something just for the sake of saving it.

In 1909, all wild animals and birds within the state of Wyoming were declared property of the state. The Wyoming State Game and Fish Department was established the same year. Therein lies another major controversy surrounding the Teton elk. The elk are owned and managed by the state, yet they summer in national parks and winter upon federal refuge lands. To complicate matters further, portions of the Jackson herd that winter on the refuge live on national forest land. And even the park elk often migrate across national forest lands to reach the refuge. This means that there are four separate government agencies responsible for the welfare of the Jackson Hole elk—the State Game and Fish Department, the National Forest Service, the National Park Service and the National Elk Refuge. Each of these agencies has its own separate ideals, philosophies and goals in dealing with the elk.

The Park Service wants the elk to exist in

as natural a setting as possible. The Forest Service doesn't want the unnaturally large numbers of elk coming from the protection of the parks to strip forest land of its vegetation, thereby causing erosion and the loss of valuable land upon which timber can be harvested and cattle grazed. The Game and Fish Department wants to see the land support a maximum number of elk so that the herd will continue to provide a huntable population. The National Elk Refuge just wants to see the herd make it through the winter intact so that the whole process can start over again. Add to this a local populace that loves the elk and makes its living from them and you have a complicated situation. The elk controversy is one reason people who used to be friends avoid each other on the boardwalks in Jackson.

Simplified, the major part of the conflict among these various agencies and the people of Jackson stems from the age-old states' rights versus federal rights debate. Many local people resent the federal government, especially the National Elk Refuge, taking care of their elk herd and telling them what to do with it. Since so many people in Jackson depend on the elk for economic means, the federal government is in a way taking care of their pocket books too. Most Jackson residents side with the State Game and Fish Department and feel that it, not the federal government, should manage the refuge. One Jacksonite told me, "There is no way you can convince me that a man sitting in Washington, D. C. knows what is best for this elk herd more than a man sitting here on the ground floor. The Department of Interior may say, yes, we are

going to save this all forever and ever. But the day may come when they won't. Just like the day may come when the state won't. But I'd rather put my bet with the state and the people in the state because they want these elk and they are going to keep them. There are so many things that can get to the federal government—budget and political pressure, mainly. The whole thing runs on money in the state department too, but so far, in Wyoming at least, we have managed to keep the politics out of our money."

Another resident added, "The old-timers, the state wardens, knew the elk. You bring in a man out of an office that's never had any experience with elk before and put him out here to manage the elk herd and he's going to make a lot of mistakes. He's bound to. The biggest mistake to date is thinking that the elk can be fed on those pellets. It's not going to work. And meanwhile there's going to be lots of elk starve to death while the government finds out it's not going to work. The federal government could maintain a herd of 25,000 to 40,000 elk if they wanted to, but they just can't afford it. The government maintains that the range is overgrazed, the same range that years ago could support as many as 50,000 elk and three times the cattle that it does today with no worry of overgrazing.

"The Wyoming Game Department and the federal government have been fighting for years. The Game Department should take over lock, stock and barrel, then you'd have one outfit managing the whole thing, except for the summer range in Yellowstone. You take a federal man and he's

Slowly but steadily, the rising temperatures thaw the frozen mountain lakes. Taken in June, this photograph shows the melting ice on Yellowstone Lake, which measures 136 square miles with an average depth of 139 feet.

transferred every two or three years. Why would he be interested in making a career of the elk and the changing problems of civilization? But the game warden, he's got a life interest in these elk, not just the hunting part but all the rest of the year too. It's the most mismanaged thing in the world."

The belief that the State Game and Fish Department could manage the elk herd is not unfounded. Not all the elk of Jackson winter upon the federal refuge. Scattered throughout the area and the state of Wyoming there are some twenty elk feeding grounds operated by the Game and Fish Department. During the winter of 1973, they fed 20,490 elk 8,748 tons of hay for a total cost of $281,000.00, which is an average of $17.00 per head. All of this was paid for by fees from the sale of elk hunting licenses.

The Game and Fish Department has even approached the Department of the Interior and asked it to relinquish management of the refuge, leaving the lands in federal ownership. In this way, the Game and Fish Department feels it could not only better manage the elk herd but also take the tax burden off of the American public and place it on Wyoming elk hunters. So far, such requests have not met with any success.

There are many reasons that the federal government will not turn the refuge over to the state. Federal officials feel that if left to the state the elk would be used primarily for economic benefit. There is some question, too, as to whether or not the Game and Fish Department would be strong enough to withstand the political pressures

that would be brought to bear. Such pressures are always present and usually come from people who wish to buy, or see donated, some of the refuge lands not used by the elk for commercial or community purposes.

The federal government also has more money available to it than state agencies. At some future date a great deal more money may be required in the preservation of these elk. Anti-hunting sentiment is growing stronger in the United States, especially in the eastern portion of the country where the majority of the voting public resides. It is probable that the issue of turning over a federal wildlife refuge to a state game and fish department would meet with overwhelming opposition on a national scale. There are simply more non-hunters with powerful lobbies in Congress than there are hunters.

There is no one answer to the various elk controversies in Jackson Hole. As one resident told me, "You know, it would take five years just to scratch the surface of the elk problem here." He is right.

In my own study I have been frustrated, confused and angered over seemingly small problems that on close inspection are really larger problems. And each problem is related to another, and yet another. It is sad, really, when scrutinizing these problems, to see all the political and human manipulations and the perplexing management decisions that shroud these elk in controversy. It is sad, too, to see how dependent on man the elk have grown. The elk exist in Jackson because man permits them to exist. He has provided protection for them in the national parks, game laws to prevent

A constant threat to the elk of Jackson Hole is the increasing demand for mountain land for use in private and commercial development. There are 4,000 acres of privately owned land within Grand Teton National Park. Demand for this private land has forced prices to more than $40,000 an acre. At such prices, the National Park Service cannot compete with commercial developers and the land is sold for homesites. The situation could force the elk farther into the back country and cut off some of their normal migratory routes.

poaching and slaughter, winter range to feed on, and if necessary, hay for them to eat. Without man the Teton elk would cease to be, at least in the large herds we know today.

Had man not originally interfered by the elimination of predators and by the taking up of the elk's winter range, the problem of the elk over-populating and how to feed them would never have arisen. But man did interfere. He did upset the delicate relationship between grass, predator and elk, and things will never be set right again. The elk of Jackson Hole will never exist in a natural situation free from the influence of man for as long as the two walk the same earth.

The Teton elk have been preserved so that people traveling through the national parks or refuge may see them. They are here for hunters to hunt. But, most of all, and probably indirectly as a result of their commercial worth, they have been preserved to remind all of us what the natural world once was. When looking at these elk we may see and feel the ancient turning of the seasons. We may see how the elk and all wildlife once fitted into the natural scheme.

I asked Don Redfearn what he thought about the herd's future. He said, "People in this valley don't want things to change. They think these things are always going to be the way they are now forever and ever. But they aren't. Things are changing. Things have changed. Things will change. All we can do is plan for the changes and hope we have done the right things by the elk."

10. SONG OF THE COW

In mid-April I began to anticipate the elk's spring migration to the high country. In the early mornings I would sit on the crest of a hill and look out over the refuge. Day after day the dawn was leaden gray. Blizzards would erupt suddenly to obscure the hills and mountains. The landscape remained unchanged from the depths of winter, a glaring white desert of snow. Red-winged blackbirds, recently returned from the south, no longer heralded spring with their song, but crouched silently in barren willow branches. Ducks and geese stood forlornly on frozen nesting waters, their beaks tucked beneath their wings. And on the refuge, the elk waited restlessly to be released from winter's grip. Filled with pent-up energy from winter's long confinement, large herds raced madly about the refuge. Often, for no visible reason, the running elk would stop abruptly, wheel, and charge off in a new direction. It was as if the elk could sense the coming of spring. It was as if they could smell it growing beneath the snow and hear it in the drips of melting ice. They seemed

Scarlet gilia tints the hillsides and sagebrush flats with delicate shades of red during the summer months.

exhilarated that winter was at last coming to an end. From my hillside I, too, waited anxiously for winter to end.

Once the snow began to leave in May, the several massive elk herds that had been forced by the feedlines and deep snow to winter together began to break up. Tired of the pellets and dried grasses, small herds drifted into the foothills in search of grass. They ranged across flatlands pockmarked with dirty white patches of melting snow and ventured into the river bottoms where the willows were budding and laced with green. Nosing among the patches of snow, the elk searched out the freshest bits of green, bit them off hungrily and then stood as if savoring the flavor. From my hillside I could look out over thousands of feeding elk. They were like tiny moving dots peppered across the landscape. And then, one day in late May, I looked down on a barren and empty refuge. As if a great wind had come overnight and blown them away like so many dried leaves, the elk were gone. They had left for the high country.

Hoping to intercept the elk somewhere along their migration routes, I walked out through the sagebrush of Antelope Flats. Just as they crossed this area in the fall coming from the mountains to the refuge, the elk would cross them coming back from the refuge to the mountains. This time, though, there would be no hunters' guns awaiting them. Only myself and a camera. While searching for fresh tracks I found a trail. The two-foot-wide path was rutted and scarred from many elk's hooves. Few of the tracks were fresh. Although the elk had moved from the main portions of the refuge, they still had not left its boundaries. Choosing a tree-covered hillside where the trail branched off in several directions, I set up my cameras. Here I returned daily to wait for the elk to begin moving. My wait lasted nearly two weeks.

Unlike the fall migration when great numbers of elk move rapidly en masse, pressed by the deepening snow and the hunting season, the spring migration is leisurely. The elk were in no hurry.

Then one morning in early June, while driving from Jackson to my observation post, eight cow elk trotted across the road and gracefully jumped a buck-rail fence to vanish in the pre-dawn blackness. As I drove, more and more elk crossed in front of me. The elk were moving. Parking my truck, I hiked through the sagebrush. Not long after I had settled down to wait for sunrise, I heard the elk coming. Their hooves made hollow thumps as they struck fallen logs. Sagebrush branches swished as they brushed passing bodies. As the sounds came closer, I realized that the elk were only a dozen yards away from where I lay concealed. Raising up inches at a time, I squinted through the camera viewfinder. In the predawn twilight the moving elk appeared as large dim shadows floating across the viewing window. There was not yet enough light to shoot. Cautiously lowering myself to the ground, I hoped that the elk had not seen or heard my movement.

Cheeks burning with cold and joints stiff from immobility, I closed my eyes and waited for sunrise. It seemed only seconds later that I snapped my eyes open with a start. A ground squirrel, only inches from my face, chittered rapidly, turned and scurried into the grass. The land was

Lupine and foxtail barley are among the flowers and grasses that dot the mountainside.

Silhouetted against rising steam from the Snake River, a cow pauses among the sagebrush of the Pot Holes, one of many areas in which elk cows stop along their spring migration routes to give birth to their calves.

bathed in warm sunlight. Sitting straight up, I expected to see the elk gone and my waiting wasted. Instead, I found myself in the middle of a group of cows. They peered at me almost unbelievingly, snorted and crashed up the hillside into the trees. For a few seconds it seemed the earth had erupted with running elk and thundering hooves. Jumping to my feet and quickly gathering up my equipment, I charged up the hillside. Ahead of me the brush crashed and I caught flashes of brown amid the white aspens. Heart pounding and gasping for breath, I scooted down the hillside hoping to intercept the elk as they left the timber. Peering through the pine branches, I was greeted with the sight for which I had waited so long.

One . . . two . . . three . . . four long lines of elk were moving slowly, single-file in front of me. Old trail-wisened cows led followed by younger cows, yearlings, spikes, calves and bulls with velvet covered knobs in place of the recently shed antlers. Winter coats, bleached nearly white by the winter sun, flashed mirror-like across the prairie. Fanning out across the landscape, the elk seemed swallowed by the peaks towering overhead and dwarfed by the vastness of the land. Mentally, I traced the routes they would take.

For many days these herds would trickle from the refuge and move toward the high ranges. They would swim rivers that were brown, choppy and dangerously swollen from run-off. They would struggle through the spring blizzards which strike with sudden savagery. They would cross the treacherous muddy bogs and the highways filled with speeding tourists heading toward

Jackson. Weak from winter, many of these elk would not finish the journey.

Driven back to the high ranges by the same ancient instincts that harken geese to return north, the elk would push into the snow-shrouded mountains where the deepest drifts linger long into July. Each day they would follow the receding snow line further up country. There is no hurry. Everywhere the land abounds with plenty. There is time to stop and linger, to feed and rest. The bulls, the barren cows and the yearlings, anxious to return to old haunts and graze on the freshly greening grasses, would break through the snow and be the first to return to the summer ranges.

Along the way on the broad sage-covered flats, in the meadows and among the aspens and pines of the lower country, the cows would stop. In these places they will bring life into the world. As the time for birth draws near, the cow will leave the small migrating herds and wander off by herself. She selects no special place. The calf is born wherever she happens to be at the moment.

For several days the cow will leave her calf only to graze and water, returning to let him wobble to his long legs and nurse. The outside world has little bearing on him. He lays attuned, yet unattached. He has no need for anything but the cow's presence, protection and nourishment. His life depends solely upon hers. Should she die, the calf's death will follow.

This seclusion permits the calf to become imprinted with the cow's special scent, and she with his. Should this bond be broken during the first few hours of life, the calf will form a "mother" attachment to nearly anything, especially a scented, mov-

ing object. Researchers have found that the separation of a cow from her calf moments after birth causes the calf to regard its human abductors as "parents." Within a few hours after birth the bond between the two is stronger. After two days the bond between mother and calf is unbreakable and will remain so until the calf is weaned.

Later, when the calf is better suited to travel, the cow will lead him to a hidden spot, perhaps a small cluster of trees close to water. There in the brush, hidden away from insects and predators, the cow will keep the calf until he is strong enough to join the herd.

Those things the calf does not know instinctively, the cow will teach him. His education is quick. It must be if he is to survive in the hostile world into which he is born. All things, four or two-legged, are his potential enemies. He is the prey, the hunted one. By the time he is several days old the calf will already know the various meanings behind the cow's barks, grunts and whistles. Accordingly, he may either drop to the ground to lay flat, chin out-stretched and very still, or trot in a dis-jointed and gangling fashion to where the cow stands. Through imitation he will learn those sounds, sights and scents which are critical to his well-being. If the scratching of a tree rubbing against another tree brings no alarm to the cow, then the calf soon learns that it is to be ignored. But should the cackling of a magpie make the cow alert and nervous, then these feelings will be transmitted to the calf.

Evolution has given the calf the basic ingredients of survival. His sensitive nose can sort out the secrets of the day and night

wafted upon the breezes, selecting out of hundreds of smells only those most important. He can smell grass beneath the snow, rain that is days away or a grizzly bear on the other side of a hill. His eyes protrude so that he may see up, down, ahead and even behind to some degree. His ears flick back and forth scanning with radar-like efficiency. No sound within the scope of several hundred yards goes unnoticed. His highly perfected senses provide a constant and ever-changing source of information

Harebells, a delightful flower as fresh-smelling as the mountain air.
Tired of standing in the hot sun, a newborn calf decides to take in a noon meal while laying in the shade of his mother. A cow will normally give birth to just one calf a year.

about the world around him.

The cow and calf will not remain in seclusion for long, for elk are by nature gregarious. When the calf is strong enough to travel, he is led to the main group of cows. From that time on, he is a herd animal. He exchanges individuality for the conformity and safety of the herd, for when the senses of ten or twenty of these animals are joined in unison there is little happening that they do not know about well in advance. In the safety of the cow herd, the calf grows strong and hardy, and begins to nibble the grasses and learn the ways of his mountain world.

During the year I spent with the elk I became very attached to the cows. Although the cow appears less magnificent than the bull, she is no less beautiful. Their long slender faces and demure eyes seem to express a quiet unassuming arrogance, overwhelming curiosity and motherly love all at once. While the bulls might be the symbol of passion and defiance, the cows have a silent dignity.

Perhaps this is because the cows, with bulging flanks swaying upon thin and delicate legs, are the foundation of the entire species. It is the cow that all winter long sustains not only herself but also the life growing within. When the herds strike out for winter or summer ranges it is not a lordly bull that leads, but an old, seasoned cow. While the bulls graze and grow antlers in the lushness of spring and summer, it is the cow that nurses and protects the calf against harm. During the fall I saw a coyote playfully harassing a herd of elk, dodging in and out amongst them, yapping and nipping at their heels like a playful dog. The

Two species that share the elk's summer ranges in Jackson Hole are the bison and trumpeter swan. There are only about fifteen bison in Grand Teton National Park. The male trumpeter, called the cob, and the female, known as the pen, mate for life. In the fall of 1974, one of the swans shown in the photograph at left was shot by a poacher.

bull quickly immersed himself in the middle of his harem of cows, shook his antlers, pawed the earth and bugled mightily. The cows then chased the intruder off.

Just as the bull's calliope-like bugling announces fall in the Jackson Hole country, so does the cow's bugling announce spring. Part scream and wail, part whistle and howl, the cow's bugle echoes over the land. Few people hear this sound and recognize it for what it is. Perhaps the cow's heralding of spring is born of the stirrings of life within her own body and her exuberance at being released from winter's long, frigid confinement. This, the song of the cow, says to all who listen that winter is over and life is renewed.

As the days grow warmer and the aspen leaves begin to unfurl and whisper in the breezes, the rains come taking the snow from the lower country and driving it to the high ridges. Following the rains, a sea of flowers spreads out over the Teton country like plush, multi-colored carpet. The earth is filled with the scurry of small animals, the air with the song of birds. Frolicking, bucking calves in tow, the cow herds begin to drift higher following the tracks of bulls and barren cows toward the high country. There, amid the lush grasses the large nursery herds of cows and calves will stay. In the fall when the rut once again begins and the first snows of winter arrive, the changing seasons and the life-cycle of the Teton elk will have turned full circle.

On that June morning as I sat watching the long, ragged lines of elk pass in front of me I was saying my farewell. With the spring migration, my year had drawn to a close. I, too, had come full circle.

11. AUTUMNS TO COME

The elk of Jackson Hole are the last living link of a forgotten era. They are all that remain of a time when herds of bison made the earth tremble, flocks of passenger pigeons obscured the sun and wilderness stretched from ocean to ocean.

Like the bison, grizzly bear, bighorn sheep and grey wolf, the elk have been very nearly swept from the face of the earth. In the Teton country the large herds have found their last stronghold against civilization. Nowhere else in the world do such concentrations of elk still exist. Nowhere else do such large elk herds still move with the rhythm of the seasons, migrating to ancient summer and winter ranges. But even here the existence of the elk is a precarious one. They can retreat no further from the effects of civilization. They are trapped in this final sanctuary, hemmed in by man's progress. And there are those who would rob the elk of even this last stronghold.

A growing population gnaws hungrily at the elk's lifeline. The timber he lives in is used for paper and lumber. The ground he

Heir to an uncertain future, a young spike bull with his first set of antlers peers from the security of his grassy bed.

walks on harbors the precious minerals needed to fuel the wheels of our cities. The stream water he drinks is good for irrigation and power. The meadows he grazes are good for livestock and are highly profitable to sell as recreational homesights. With every logging road pushed into the national forests, with every plot of ground sold for commercial development, with every new campground opened for the swelling numbers of tourists, with every new trail created for hikers, some portion of the elk's wilderness dies. Some portion of the ground he needs to winter and summer upon or travel through is lost forever.

The elk of Jackson Hole are at a critical crossroads. They are pawns in a powerful game of chess between those who wish to preserve America's natural heritage and those who wish to destroy it. It is a game played by hunters, backpackers, realtors, tourists, ranchers, conservationists, politicians, and state and federal agencies. It is a game played for keeps, and in its outcome rests not just the future of this elk herd, but the preservation of every portion of North America's wilderness and the wildlife it harbors. For when these last great elk herds begin to die, can the other herds of elk scattered throughout the continent and the many other species of wildlife be far behind? The Jackson Hole elk have the protection of two great national parks and a federal refuge. They are recipients of winter feeding, expensive programs of study and the wholehearted support of an entire nation. Yet, if they cease to exist, can other species be expected to persevere?

If, on the other hand, man should find a way to peacefully co-exist with these elk

These elk delight in a splashing, springtime dip in a mountain stream, unconcerned with the future. But because of their fragile environment, I wonder about autumns to come.

herds, let them move naturally as they have for thousands of years and preserve them for other than commercial benefit, then could he not find a way to also live with the grizzly bear, grey wolf, bighorn sheep and other wildlife?

Within the next decade, the fate of these elk will be determined. Never before have the policies of wilderness and wildlife conservationists been so staunchly and fiercely challenged. Never has the existence of true wilderness been so threatened.

If we allow the fragile environment of the Jackson Hole elk to be damaged and the elk herds to drift into oblivion, we will have lost something more than the elk. We will have lost a vital part of ourselves.

I hope always that in the fall I may climb to the high ridges and sit among the yellowed meadows to listen for the bull's ancient song of mountain autumn. I hope to always see the elk massed by the thousands on their winter range. I want to be able to walk among the flowers of spring and see the cows with tumbling, bucking calves at their sides. For me, the kind of world in which I would live and raise my children and grandchildren would not be one in which there was not enough room for the Teton elk.

SUGGESTED READING

I have not attempted a comprehensive bibliography, but rather a list of books that I feel will aid the reader who wishes to know more about elk and the Jackson Hole region.

In 1927, Olaus Murie, then a young biologist for the United States Bureau of Biological Survey, was detailed to Jackson Hole to make a thorough study of the elk herds. Often Mr. Murie would take his wife, Mardy, and their children with him as he packed into the remote back country. The result of his many years of study was published in 1951 by Stackpole Press under the title *The Elk of North America*. It remains today, in my opinion, the most comprehensive work ever done on elk. Mr. Murie later accepted the directorship of the Wilderness Society, but only on the terms that he would be able to stay in his beloved Teton country. His death was a great loss to all who value the preservation of wilderness and wildlife.

Mardy Murie lives in Jackson. My wife Alisa and I were fortunate to have been able to visit with her several times. She is a warm and wonderful person—an inspiration to all young people interested in conservation. Mr. and Mrs. Murie wrote *Wapiti Wilderness*, Knopf, 1969, about the people, animals and mountains of Jackson and illustrated with Olaus' sketches. This book is one of my favorites.

Others that I would include on this list are:

Anderson, Chester C., *The Elk of Jackson Hole*, The Wyoming Game and Fish Commission, Cheyenne, Wyoming, 1958. An out-of-print paperback, this is a review of Jackson Hole elk studies. For the serious student of elk, it is a must.

Calkins, Frank, *Jackson Hole*, Knopf, New York, 1972. Sprinkled with Mr. Calkins' dry humor, this book is a comprehensive and highly enjoyable study of Jackson Hole's past, present and future.

Fryxell, Fritiof, *The Tetons—Interpretations of a Mountain Landscape*, University of California Press, Berkeley and Los Angeles, 1966. A must for understanding the geologic history of the Tetons and Jackson Hole and its bearing upon the weather and wildlife.

Hough, Donald, *Snow Above Town*, Norton, New York, 1943. A humorous personal account of living in Jackson Hole before it became a booming tourist resort.

Hunter, Rodello, *Wyoming Wife*, Knopf, New York, 1969. A woman's view of living in the Jackson area, this book contains some delicious recipes, as Rodello is a terrific "mountain" cook.

Newhall, Nancy, *The Tetons and Yellowstone*, The Five Associates, Redwood City, California, 1970. A concise, almost poetic description of Jackson Hole's history, illustrated with excellent reproductions of Ansel Adams' photographs. During the summer that I began working on my book, Mrs. Newhall died as the result of a rafting accident on the Snake River near Jackson. Mrs. Newhall loved the Teton country and her loss is deeply felt by all who treasure the western wildernesses.

Sutton, Ann and Myron, *Yellowstone, A Century of the Wilderness Idea*, Macmillan Company, New York, and the Yellowstone Library and Museum Association, 1972. Good reading and a beautiful description of the northernmost portions of Jackson Hole's elk ranges and the ideals behind the preservation of wilderness. Illustrated with photographs by Charles Stienhacker.

SEASON OF THE ELK

was designed by David E. Spaw,
photocomposed in Trump Mediaeval,
and printed on Warren's Flokote Enamel
by
The Lowell Press, Kansas City, Missouri